U.S. POLICY TOWARD CHINA

Other Books in the At Issue Series:

Affirmative Action
Business Ethics
Domestic Violence
Environmental Justice
Ethnic Conflict
Immigration Policy
Legalizing Drugs
The Media and Politics
Policing the Police
Rape on Campus
Smoking
What Is Sexual Harassment?

U.S. POLICY TOWARD CHINA

David Bender, *Publisher*

Bruno Leone, *Executive Editor*

Scott Barbour, *Managing Editor*

Brenda Stalcup, *Series Editor*

Charles P. Cozic, *Book Editor*

An Opposing Viewpoints ® Series

Greenhaven Press, Inc.
San Diego, California

Library of Congress Cataloging-in-Publication Data

U.S. policy toward China / Charles P. Cozic, book editor.
     p.   cm. — (At issue) (An opposing viewpoints series)
     Includes bibliographical references and index.
     ISBN 1-56510-389-0 (alk. paper). — ISBN 1-56510-388-2 (pbk. : alk. paper).
     1. United States—Foreign relations—China. 2. China—Foreign relations—United States. I. Cozic, Charles P., 1957-   . II. Series: Opposing viewpoints series (Unnumbered). III. Series.
E183.8.C5A7235   1996
327.73051—dc20   95-24182
                                                                   CIP

© 1996 by Greenhaven Press, Inc., PO Box 289009,
San Diego, CA 92198-9009

Printed in the U.S.A.

Table of Contents

Page

Introduction   7

1. America Should Mix Cooperation with Confrontation Toward China   10
   David Zweig

2. Renewing China's Most-Favored-Nation Status Benefits Both Nations   23
   Bill Clinton

3. America Should Maintain Most-Favored-Nation Status for a Stronger China   26
   Bryce Harland

4. U.S. Policy Should Stress Trade with China   30
   Robert Kapp

5. U.S. Policy Should Not Link Trade to Chinese Human Rights Protection   34
   James Finn

6. U.S.-Chinese Cooperation Strengthens Asia-Pacific Security   38
   William Perry

7. America and China Should Cooperate to Protect Intellectual Property Rights   44
   Wu Yi

8. Bill Clinton Should Not Have Renewed China's Most-Favored-Nation Status   49
   The Progressive

9. China's Most-Favored-Nation Status Should Be Revoked   52
   Fang Lizhi

10. U.S. Policy Should Stress Chinese Human Rights Protection   55
    Mike Jendrzejczyk

11. U.S. Policy Tolerates China's Wrongdoings   64
    William P. Hoar

12. America Should Prepare for China's Military Threat   69
    Thomas L. McNaugher

13. The United States Should Crack Down on Chinese Espionage   78
    Malcolm McConnell

14. China Is Unlikely to Protect American Intellectual Property Rights   83
    Frankie Fook-lun Leung

Organizations to Contact   86

Bibliography   90

Index   93

Introduction

On June 19, 1995, Chinese authorities arrested American citizen Harry Wu on charges of spying, an act punishable by death. Wu, a Chinese-born human rights activist, had entered China to investigate human rights abuses in the communist nation's *laogai* (prison system). During previous trips to China, Wu had gathered evidence of what he alleged was slave labor by approximately ten million prisoners at more than one thousand forced labor camps, including the manufacture of goods exported to America. For nineteen years, Wu himself had been imprisoned in the *laogai* for criticizing China's support of the Soviet Union's 1956 invasion of Hungary.

Following Wu's arrest, human rights activists and the U.S. government protested vehemently and demanded Wu's immediate release. According to the *Washington Post*, the filing of criminal charges against Wu amounted to "a test of the whole relationship between the United States and China." On August 24, 1995, China relented and expelled Wu from the country.

The Tiananmen Square massacre

Wu's arrest came two weeks after the sixth anniversary of another test of U.S.-China relations: the June 1989 Tiananmen Square massacre, in which Chinese troops crushed a prodemocracy/proreform demonstration in Beijing by indiscriminately shooting and killing hundreds of college students and other demonstrators. In the aftermath of the crackdown, many Americans expressed outrage and insisted that the United States impose economic sanctions to punish the Chinese government.

Human rights activists and other Americans urged the United States to revoke China's most-favored-nation (MFN) trade status. Reviewed annually according to U.S. law, MFN affords China, the world's eleventh-largest trading nation, the same tariff treatment as most other U.S. trading partners. Without MFN, China could lose billions of dollars in trade with the United States. China is the fourth-largest exporter of goods to America, and much of its economy is dependent on U.S. trade. With exports to America four times greater than imports, China derived a surplus of nearly $30 billion from U.S. trade in 1994.

By revoking MFN, activists and others maintained, America could send a powerful message to China's leaders that brutal acts such as the Tiananmen Square massacre would not be tolerated. In addition, they asserted that such a move would hurt China economically and thereby force it to hold human rights in higher regard. However, MFN has been renewed each year since the massacre. In 1993, Bill Clinton attached a condition of human rights progress to the annual renewal of MFN, but he withdrew the proviso one year later, announcing that China had made "overall, significant progress."

Human rights are paramount

Many commentators continue to criticize China's human rights record. In January 1995, Winston Lord, assistant U.S. secretary of state for East Asian and Pacific affairs, declared, "Frankly, on the human rights front, the situation has deteriorated. They're rounding up dissidents, harassing them more." One month later, the U.S. State Department proclaimed that China's human rights record was bleaker than ever, with continuing "widespread and well documented" violations of "internationally accepted norms." Human rights activists point out that China's communist government denies its people three avenues to improved human rights: an independent judicial system to challenge the government; a free press; and grassroots nongovernmental groups, which are outlawed.

Some continue to press for the removal of China's MFN status. In May 1995, one such advocate, Frank R. Wolf, a Republican member of the U.S. House of Representatives, told the House Ways and Means Subcommittee on Trade that China's human rights violations were egregious. Wolf argued that in addition to forced prison labor, China compels women to undergo abortions and sterilizations under its one-child-per-couple population control policy. Wolf also testified that Chinese authorities are trafficking human organs taken from executed prisoners and that "human fetuses are being sold as health food in government-run hospitals and private clinics."

These and other charges against China have caused many U.S. companies to reconsider conducting business there. At least two—Levi-Strauss and Timberland—regard human rights in China more important than profitable ventures. In 1993, both companies terminated operations in China, citing pervasive human rights violations. According to Orville Schell, a senior fellow at Columbia University's Freedom Forum, "Unless you think humankind survives by commerce alone, you cannot but be alarmed at the bleakness of China spiritually, culturally, and politically."

Keeping business and trade in mind

In response to demands that China be punished for violating human rights, many observers have countered that America's economic ties should be maintained or strengthened in order to let China's growing market economy produce improved human rights. They argue that through trade, joint ventures, and other business arrangements, American-style capitalism—and Western values of democracy and freedom—will take root and eventually permeate Chinese society. Upon renewing MFN in May 1994, Bill Clinton remarked that trade "offers us the best opportunity to lay the basis for long-term sustainable progress on human rights." According to Kent Wiedemann, a U.S. deputy assistant secretary of state, "Through trade, U.S. concepts filter into the consciousness of all Chinese. Opening markets for America's idea industries [compact discs, computer software, and movies] . . . spread U.S. values and ideals."

A growing number of U.S. companies, attracted by plentiful, cheap labor and other incentives, have entered into partnerships with Chinese businesspeople. Lino Piedra, director of international affairs for the

Chrysler Corporation, argues that these joint ventures benefit Chinese society: "In a joint venture, the only option is to be there or not be there, and by being there our standards and Western influences contribute to social progress."

Many business and foreign policy experts contend that America's business ties with China are too important to allow every issue of human rights to jeopardize the relationship. They also disagree that U.S. companies should play a strong role in improving human rights in China. United States–China Business Council analyst Dan Martin went so far as to say, "It should not be the burden of the business community to fix human rights abuses." Piedra adds, "Unless we went on some sort of scavenger hunt all over China, how can we check out all of a [joint venture] partner's operations?" In the business community and elsewhere, some Americans argue that U.S. criticism of human rights abuses amounts to hypocrisy. According to the *South China Morning Post*, media mogul Ted Turner "told a conference in Hong Kong that countries such as the United States should look to their own problems before criticizing China for its human rights record."

Whether they are more supportive of human rights or of business in China, many people acknowledge the significance of China as an economic partner and the importance of good relations with the Asian power. Some believe that these factors outweigh concern for human rights. According to *Newsday* columnist Robert Reno: "The U.S. corporate presence in China has become so huge and so lucrative that the time for talking about punishing China for being beastly to its dissidents has long past." Some experts suggest that because of the extent of this presence, the U.S. government is unlikely to be adamant about improved human rights conditions.

In March 1995, the Clinton administration considered recommendations from both human rights activists and business leaders and lobbyists when it drafted a voluntary code of conduct for U.S. businesses operating abroad. The code, not specifically mentioning China, asks U.S. business leaders to set a good example by refusing to allow discrimination in the workplace and respecting the right of free association and collective bargaining. Whether this code has a positive effect on human rights remains to be seen.

The question of whether U.S. policy should stress human rights or economic engagement with China is the main focus of *At Issue: U.S. Policy Toward China*. Many of the viewpoints in this anthology were written in anticipation of Clinton's 1994 decision on whether or not to renew China's MFN status; the authors present cogent arguments for and against linking the issues of human rights and trade. Other viewpoints discuss China's potential military threat, the protection of American intellectual property rights, and other issues that affect U.S.-Chinese relations.

1

America Should Mix Cooperation with Confrontation Toward China

David Zweig

David Zweig is an associate professor of international relations at the Fletcher School of Law and Diplomacy at Tufts University in Medford, Massachusetts.

Relations with China in the near and distant future will be problematic for the United States. American interests include democratization and improved human rights in China, increased trade between both nations, and the containment of Chinese weapons and nuclear technology. These objectives can be achieved through economic, political, and cultural cooperation mixed with direct confrontation on issues such as human rights, arms sales, unfair trade, and nuclear proliferation.

In devising a policy toward China, President Bill Clinton's administration faces a series of important questions. The president's overall foreign policy goals are relatively clear: promote democracy and freedom worldwide, resuscitate the American economy and America's international economic strength, and ensure American and global security. But what should be the hierarchy among these issues? Should one issue dominate? Can one pursue all three at the same time and still maximize the national interest?

The end of the cold war has drastically reduced American concerns with military security while increasing those regarding economic issues. Clinton was elected president precisely because he could best articulate the American public's anxiety about the changing global economic environment. No doubt, he also reflects concerns with human rights and democratization that are deep within the American body politic. But right

David Zweig, "Clinton and China: Creating a Policy Agenda That Works." Reprinted with permission from *Current History* magazine (September 1993); ©1993, Current History, Inc.

now, Americans want jobs and a better position in the global marketplace.

And herein lies the problem. Economic growth, particularly trade-based growth, is an interdependent process; without markets for exports, there is no growth, and without imports there is no comparative advantage. If pursuing a foreign policy based on expanding human rights globally undermines access to markets, leads to large increases in the prices Americans pay for goods, and complicates security relations with a major global and regional power, what is a president to do?

The lack of a clear hierarchy is not the only problem confronting a president who must govern in an interdependent world. The tools of his trade, the weapons of statecraft, have changed as well. As he moves into the realm of economic policy, Clinton will rapidly discover that America's military power is not the key determinant of bilateral policy conflicts, especially those involving economic issues. (If it were, the United States could, for example, use its superior military might to force the Japanese to open their markets.) In the case of China, the leverage to make it respond to United States concerns is based more on the degree to which China needs access to American markets, investment, and technology. How long it would take China to find new markets and the costs of doing so greatly enhance the leverage the United States has over China.

But can one successfully use economic power to affect another state's political agenda? Can influence in one area be used to affect outcomes in another? As the president contemplated his decision on whether or not to grant China most favored nation (MFN) status in 1993, whether to apply conditions to it, and how to deal with China for the rest of his administration, he found that those issues clouded the horizon. [The United States decides MFN status each spring. Clinton linked human rights conditions to MFN renewal in 1993, but removed them in 1994.] If he withdrew MFN, what would have been the effect on the United States economy? How many American jobs would be lost? What would have been the impact on the price of basic consumer goods? How to calculate the opportunity costs to American businesses—to the economy—if the United States were the only country excluded from competition in the fastest growing economy in the world? Moreover, with the United States trying to legitimize the role of the UN as a regional peacekeeper, could the United States afford bad ties with a rising global power, one that is a permanent member of the Security Council? Yet without threatening China's economic growth, without using America's most potent leverage over China—access to the United States market—how could he also press forward his goal of bringing greater freedom to the people of China?

What does America want from China?

America's agenda toward China is based on what the United States wants from that country. One can start from the assumption that American foreign policy should serve American interests. But what are United States interests in China?

Let us start with the tough ones, human rights and democratization. Many constituencies in the United States, including the president, liberal and conservative members of Congress, human rights groups, Chinese students, and perhaps many average American citizens, are particularly exercised by the human rights abuses, mistreatment of prisoners, repression in Tibet, and arrests of political activists that continue to occur in China. But why do Americans care whether China turns democratic and throws off its Communist mantle? First, a democratic China would ensure the same high standard of human rights for its citizens that Americans have. It is a fundamental belief among Americans that the Chinese should have the right to speak their minds on political issues without fear of incarceration. Second, because democracies have internal restraints on military expansion, it is assumed that a democratic China would be a peaceful China, which would help guarantee the security of China's neighbors and the United States. Third, it is assumed that a democratic China would be more stable politically, easier to negotiate with, and more likely to fulfill its global commitments on issues such as arms control and nonproliferation, environmental degradation, and population control.

> *It is a fundamental belief among Americans that the Chinese should have the right to speak their minds on political issues without fear of incarceration.*

While some of these assumptions are questionable—could a democratic China stem the rapid growth of the country's population?—we must still ask a basic question: how fast do we want change to occur in China? And what are the risks involved in pushing for rapid change? Some members of the United States Congress believe that the collapse of the Chinese Communist party will lead to a democratic alternative. However, the most likely scenario would be a takeover by a Chinese military no longer constrained by a Communist party. This could be even more destabilizing for the region, since there would be little internal opposition to further expansion of the military budget. One of paramount leader Deng Xiaoping's greatest contributions to regional stability in the 1980s was the demilitarization of Chinese society and China's foreign policy. Only in the wake of Tiananmen, when the military saved the regime, has it successfully flexed its political muscle to get a larger share of the national budget.[1] The collapse of the party could also exacerbate human rights abuses—witness the cruelty meted out during the post-Tiananmen crackdown to those who were arrested by the martial law troops.

An alternative scenario would be the situation that has emerged in the former Soviet Union. When freedom suddenly explodes without the development of proper political institutions, political chaos is likely. But where will the United States be when China tries to put the pieces of a collapsed system back together? Look how slowly the United States has responded to the needs of the former Soviet republics. Unlike the Soviet Union, which was a direct military threat to the United States, China does not directly threaten American security. A collapse leading to chaos may be of less benefit to the United States than such an outcome was in the former Soviet Union. Collapse and disorder could trigger a massive flow of refugees into Hong Kong, or a new stream of boat people onto the shores of Japan, South Korea, and Taiwan. While Deng has raised this fear to frighten the world into not pressing China for political reform, one cannot underestimate the costs to all of East Asia if internal chaos in China demolishes the floodgates controlling more than one billion people.

Yet, if the United States does not press the Chinese to adopt democratic institutions for China's own benefit, China will continue its cycle of liberalizations and crackdowns, which alienate the population and undermine economic growth. Without strong popular institutions, China's leaders increase the possibility of chaos when the political system does weaken further, which it eventually will. No doubt, rapid economic growth and expanding income inequality are placing great pressures on the Chinese system. But what type of system can best handle these strains? While Westerners believe democratic institutions are the solution, the examples of Singapore, Taiwan, and South Korea lead many Chinese to believe in the utility of a "new authoritarianism" that would maintain stability as the country goes through its rapid growing pains. (In fact, one more decade of political authoritarianism and rapid economic growth may be the perfect formula for the emergence of a moderately wealthy, politically modern Chinese state.)

But the 1980s also shows that without stable, reliable institutions through which people can express their concerns about official corruption, unequal development, and fears of inflation, the Chinese people, especially students, will take to the streets and subvert political stability. It is therefore in everyone's interests to press the Chinese government to gradually create real institutions for the democratic expression of popular concerns.

America's economic agenda with China

In Bill Clinton's search for a formula to reinvigorate the United States economy in the short term and strengthen its underlying qualities in the long term, China will be an important element. The United States has become more export-oriented, in search of new international markets. Since China will become the fastest growing market in the world in the next twenty years, United States firms must be able to sell their goods there. Bilateral trade has expanded dramatically; by 1992 China was America's ninth-largest trading partner. Trade soared that year, with the United States exporting $7.5 billion to China, and China exporting $25.7 billion to the United States. China's direct exports to the United States account for 9.2 percent of total Chinese exports, a figure that continues to grow.

As the quality of China's work force improves, American firms must consider offshore production in China a necessary part of their Asian economic development strategies. However, the president's agenda of increasing jobs at home may run counter to such strategies. But as more and more of America's competitors for market share in East Asia use China's labor force to produce higher quality products at relatively low prices, American firms will have to follow suit. Even the president's desire to increase the number of higher value added and high-tech jobs at home runs counter to market forces that will pull United States producers of technological products into China.[2]

The United States also needs cheap Chinese exports to keep the price of its own goods down. Personal income in the United States is declining as more and more people shift from higher paying manufacturing jobs to lower paying service sector jobs. But lower salaries need not lead to a lower standard of living if the costs of Chinese-made household appliances decline as well.

But the United States also wants fair trade with China. While it imports billions of dollars of Chinese goods, the United States also wants access to China's more than one billion consumers. The Commerce Department and the United States trade representative pushed the Chinese to sign a Memorandum of Understanding (MOU) on market access in October 1992, which will greatly reduce tariff barriers on hundreds of goods.

Other obstacles remain, however, including protecting American copyrights and intellectual property. American trade unions also want an end to prison labor exports to the United States, which contravene United States trade laws such as Section 307 of the 1930 Tariff Act. These latter issues loom as potential points of confrontation in the trade realm.

The international agenda with China

A broad set of global issues also shape United States policy toward China. At the top of this list is the desire that China stop selling long- and medium-range missiles to countries in unstable regions and to enemies of American allies, such as Syria. China, which has agreed to abide by the Missile Technology Control Regime (MTCR), has a moral obligation to restrict its missile sales. The United States would like China to be far more circumspect in transferring nuclear technology, especially to countries, such as Iran and Algeria, that are trying to build nuclear weapons, and it desperately wants the Chinese not to employ military measures to resolve its territorial claim on Taiwan. For decades Taiwan has been a divisive issue in American politics; should the People's Republic resort to force, the United States would find itself in a situation where it might have to intervene.

For financial reasons, the United States hopes that Britain will successfully transfer sovereignty over Hong Kong to China in 1997 and that China will not destabilize the Hong Kong economy. The United States has over 60,000 expatriates living in Hong Kong and is the colony's third-largest investor, after China and Japan. As a measure of its concern, the United States Congress has passed legislation calling on China to resolve the transfer of sovereignty in a prudent manner. Under the 1992 United States–Hong Kong Policy Act, the secretary of state is to monitor Hong Kong's democratic institutions, while the president is to ensure that they function autonomously after China takes over.

On issues of East Asian security, the United States needs high-level Chinese cooperation if any kind of regional arrangement is to be built. Unless there is international cooperation in East Asia, a new era of nationalism will emerge. And President Clinton may see a regional security arrangement as one way to decrease American military obligations in East Asia, which are a drain on the economy.

As the United States contemplates building this East Asian security system, it must deal with a "rising China," whose economy is growing rapidly and whose military is in a stronger position domestically than at any time since 1971.[3] The rapid growth of China's GNP [gross national product] will put more funds in the hands of the Chinese military. Con-

in the late 1970s, it again faced international opprobrium after crushing the pro-democracy movement in Tiananmen in 1989. China is thus highly sensitive about its international stature and strongly wants to take what it sees as its rightful place near the top of the community of nations.

Two events are high on China's international agenda, and both give the United States some leverage. First, China's entrance into the General Agreement on Tariffs and Trade (GATT) passes through Washington, and the Chinese know it. One of the terms of 1992's MOU on market access was that the United States would work "enthusiastically" for China's entry into GATT. But the visit of Assistant United States Trade Representative for GATT Affairs Douglas Newkirk to Beijing, where he said that China would probably not gain access to GATT for at least another five to seven years, created great consternation in the Chinese government. Linking criticism of China's restrictive trading practices and its ability to gain entrance into GATT is one way for the United States to press China to further lower its tariff barriers.

China also strongly desires to host the Olympics in the [future]. Billboards throughout Beijing exhort the people to present a good face in order not to undermine China's chances of being the site of the Olympics. While the United States has no veto in the International Olympic Committee, American pressure against China's hosting the Olympics could be problematic.

Finally, while the Chinese would never admit that they need help in solving an issue deemed an "internal affair," they do need the United States to maintain its "One China Policy," and its pressure on Taiwan not to seek independence. Recent conferences by China scholars and presentations before congressional hearings have called on the people of Taiwan to remain patient. For China, a declaration of independence by Taiwan would be the worst possible scenario; the inevitable use of military force would, at the very least, scuttle the current economic boom.

Pursuing the foreign policy agenda

While the United States needs to confront China directly on an array of critical issues, American political leaders must not jettison the relationship because China pursues its own interests in a manner that challenges world trends. They must confront that behavior and work to affect it. The best strategy for the Clinton administration is a mixed strategy that combines efforts at strategic enmeshment; continued economic, cultural, and political involvement, which will allow the United States to benefit from the "open door" China cannot afford to close; and direct confrontations on human rights, arms sales, unfair trade, and nuclear proliferation when China's actions are inimical to United States global and national interests. The "easier" partner of the mid-1980s is gone for now, but one should not assume that a mix of quiet diplomacy, public protestations, and hard negotiations cannot gain results.

As has been noted, China's trade dependency on the United States market leaves China highly vulnerable to American trade pressures. If China lost access to the United States market, its economic boom, particularly in south China, would stumble badly. No other market of similar proportions exists for its exports. Foreign investment that relies on re-exports to the United States would also decrease. But the degree of vulnerability for both the United States and China varies across policy arenas. The United States has great leverage when directly confronting China over specific economic and trade policies. And United States firms benefit from trade pressures that improve access to the Chinese market. For a president who must worry about jobs, directly challenging China to open its market [by] using clear guidelines and indicators of compliance may be a far more effective strategy than a broadside on the trade relationship because of a political agenda. Even Clinton has recognized that the Bush administration's strategy of threatening economic sanctions to gain movement on economic policies, rather than using economic threats for political purposes, has led to significant agreements with China on a host of economic issues, including MOUs on prison labor, intellectual property rights, and market access.

Still, implementation mechanisms and monitoring systems are a problem, since Beijing appears unwilling or unable to enforce these commitments. The United States trade representative must continue to pressure the Chinese to meet agreements they have made under the MOUs. The Voice of America [U.S. government radio broadcasts] must play a role in informing local officials of the content of these agreements—the Chinese government, it seems, may not fully inform local governments of their obligations under the MOUs—and consular officials must meet with local trade officials and warn them that their export market is at risk if they do not conform to these agreements. The Chinese must be warned that if direct, issue-specific trade negotiations do not open China's markets, lower the trade imbalance, and end trade violations, pressure could build in the United States for widespread trade confrontations. Asia scholar Ross Munro has suggested a trade agreement that would compel China to increase its imports from, or decrease its exports to, the United States whenever China's trade surplus approached a target zone. Such "managed trade" may not be unwelcome by the current United States trade representative.

Conditional MFN: the thin edge of the wedge

How can the United States push its agenda of improving China's human rights behavior? Was making MFN conditional in 1993 the right strategy? There are enormous economic costs and political risks in linking MFN to China's human rights behavior. If MFN is ended because China does not meet the human rights conditions, China could raise tariffs from the "minimum" category to the "general" category for a host of United States [exports] and shift to other suppliers from Europe and Japan. The American aircraft industry, producers of chemical fertilizer, exporters of wheat and other grains, and producers of industrial and construction machinery would suffer most. These four industries comprise much of the $7.5 billion in imports China bought from the United States in 1992. The United States–China Business Council estimates that ending MFN would cost 100,000 United States jobs, a difficult pill to swallow for a president who has made employment expansion "job one." Hong Kong, as Governor Christopher Patten told the president, would suffer badly, since many of its products exported to the United States are now produced in mainland

China and would therefore face much stiffer tariffs in the United States market. Similarly, many Taiwanese and Korean firms producing offshore on the Chinese mainland would be forced to relocate to other parts of Southeast Asia.

Second, few in the United States business community support linking trade policies and human rights. This community believes that expanding business is a liberating force in itself. Moreover, the examples of Taiwan and South Korea suggest that economic development and the creation of free markets help generate support for democratic transitions. One potential fallacy in this argument, however, is the assumption that economic development inevitably leads to the creation of an autonomous middle class, which then presses the state for political liberalization. In China, where private property rights are still unclear, much of the economic growth is due to local government industrialization, which may weaken the central state's control over the localities, but need not generate a middle class, as it has in South Korea and Taiwan.

Third, jeopardizing trade relations for improvements in Chinese domestic behavior is risky. By making MFN conditional, the president will be in a bind not to appear weak on human rights: unless China makes *very* significant progress, it will be hard for him to certify that it has. This fact will shift the debate to whether or not to withdraw MFN. The political stakes and pressures at that time will dwarf anything we have seen to date in the recurrent discussions on MFN. Also, given the current pace of economic growth, the problems in rural China, and growing inequalities and corruption, major protests could reemerge in the next twelve months. China will meet that challenge forcefully, and if necessary with brutality. No doubt, massive arrests of peaceful demonstrators and secret executions of labor activists, as in 1989, would and should not be tolerated; but should we condemn China for trying to maintain some semblance of social order as it undergoes this historic growth spurt? And tying MFN to China's domestic behavior, rather than to external acts such as arms sales which the central government should be able to control, puts the initiative in the hands of people who want to see MFN taken away. One might anticipate massive riots in Tibet next spring as young monks become aware that triggering a military crackdown in Tibet will force the president's hand to end MFN. [China has sovereignty over Tibet, an autonomous region.]

One should not assume that a mix of quiet diplomacy, public protestations, and hard negotiations cannot gain results.

Fourth, despite the president's desire to preserve Sino-American ties, conditional MFN will undermine bilateral business relations. In the eyes of businessmen in both China and the United States, conditional MFN may have been the first step down the slippery slope of taking away MFN, given that 1994's debate will not be about imposing conditions but instead will focus on whether or not to remove MFN altogether. So conditional MFN dramatically increases the risk for Americans of doing business in China. Similarly, Chinese businessmen may hesitate to establish joint ventures with American firms, now that the United States administration is one step closer to canceling MFN. Two years ago, an American businesswoman could not get the best silk producer in Nantong to meet with her; he felt that the possible withdrawal of MFN made working with American firms too risky. Today many Chinese firms must perceive the risks to be even higher.

While threatening to withdraw MFN may appear to be the best tool, doing so will undermine the leverage the United States has over China.

It is continued economic engagement that keeps China trapped in its tango with the United States. Without access to the United States market, China could not grow as rapidly as it has, but without that engagement the United States would have less leverage over China's internal affairs. While threatening to withdraw MFN may appear to be the best tool, doing so will undermine the leverage the United States has over China. But because of the linkage between economic growth and the United States market, China cannot disengage from the United States, even as the United States presses China on human rights, democratization, and arms control. Moreover, continued economic expansion will allow for the slow emergence of social forces—the civil society—that may eventually lead to a democratic transition. External pressure can create the context within which liberalization will occur, but unless society is ripe, as it was in South Korea in 1988 when hosting the Olympics prevented the Korean military from cracking down on popular protests, it cannot be the critical force triggering democratic change.[5]

Moreover, prodding China to release political prisoners and build democratic institutions is far short of making human rights the pillar of United States policy toward China. In the current context, where American popular opinion, presidential views, and congressional concerns so strongly favor democratization in China, support for a "peaceful evolution" of the Chinese political system seems the most appropriate public policy. According to a recent suggestion from the Atlantic Council and the National Committee on United States–China Relations, a bilateral human rights commission may be one useful forum for a "quiet dialogue on human rights at senior levels." The United States government should also press China in many multilateral forums, such as the UN Human Rights Commission, to improve its human rights record. It should use the Voice of America as a tool to help Chinese understand the outside world. It must engage government officials and Chinese research scholars in a debate about the benefits of democratization, and the opportunities that exist for peaceful transitions that leave ruling parties in power—noting that this has been the outcome in Taiwan and South Korea. But Americans must also make it clear that they call for liberalization in order to avoid the breakdown of political authority in China, not to trigger it. Given China's experience of the past ninety years, few Chinese, outside a sector of intellectuals and working class activists, support foreign efforts to destabilize their country. A gentler, less corrupt and more equitable system with rising incomes would satisfy most Chinese today.

Despite the important constraints imposed on United States China policy, events may not follow the logic dictated by this theory for several reasons. First, ideological commitment to human rights by the president, plus his need to maintain strong ties to his party's liberal wing, led him to [originally] favor conditional MFN. But using an executive order warning China about its human rights and arms proliferation abuses to replace congressional legislation conditioning MFN has created the perception that this is a declaratory policy with too few teeth for a president who sharply criticized the former administration on its policy, and who needs the support of Congress for his domestic agenda. Second, China's own behavior, especially its inability to abide by its pledges and legal commitments not to sell intermediate-range missiles, fuels the furor in Washington against China. Third, the inconsistency between United States political and economic ties with China complicates the relationship. In the past the two were always in balance: in the 1950s the United States and China hated each other and had no trade; in the 1970s the two nations were cautiously interactive both politically and economically; the mid-1980s saw the heyday of political, military and economic ties. But since Tiananmen, political ties have remained at best cool, while economic ties have heated up. But American foreign policy often struggles with such dissonance; efforts by politicians to bridge this moral and economic gap will cause them to restrict economic ties.

A careful policy that asserts American and global interests can succeed, if the United States is patient and has the will to pursue it.

On the Taiwan issue, the administration must recognize that despite the numerous Sino-American confrontations since the 1950s centering on Taiwan, Americans have consistently underestimated the importance of Taiwan to the Chinese government. Despite an apparent amelioration in relations with Taiwan, the Chinese government will not tolerate an independent Taiwan; and if an invasion follows a declaration of independence, the United States will be forced to confront the Chinese militarily. Thus, while it asserts that it has no position on this "internal affair" between the Chinese, the real challenge for the United States will come if Taiwan proclaims its independence.

Finally, if we are to arrest China's possible expansion into the South China Sea, work for a peaceful solution to the Taiwan issue, prevent a Sino-Japanese arms race, and establish some kind of security arrangement in East Asia, the United States must be involved in direct talks with the Chinese military. The Chinese cannot dismiss American and Asian concerns about an expanding Chinese military by innocent protestations of misunderstanding. China's "peaceful" and "just" foreign policy positions (as the Chinese call them) are not apparent to all. Serious concerns are emerging about Chinese great power aspirations, and until China responds to those issues through greater openness, there should be no lifting of the sales embargo on "dual use" technology. An engaged United States policy, which tries to enmesh the Chinese military in a stronger bilateral or preferably multilateral security arrangement, rather than one that seeks to dismantle China's Communist system, will garner strong support from America's Asian friends.

Dealing with China in the near and distant future will not be easy. A system under stress—with weak political institutions, a succession looming, and with dramatically different cultural traditions—will continue to challenge American policymakers. But strong economic ties can limit China's freedom of movement, even as they limit America's own. A careful policy that asserts American and global interests can succeed, if the United States is patient and has the will to pursue it.

Notes

1. It is also important to remember that the Persian Gulf War, with its display of American military technology, heightened the Chinese military's awareness of the great technical gap between it and the Western militaries. Some of the growth in defense spending must be seen as a response to these concerns for national security, rather than simply seen as reflecting Chinese expansionist tendencies.

2. It is estimated that there are at least 50,000 highly talented software engineers in China; Taiwanese and Japanese firms have already begun to forge close links with Chinese software firms. If American businesses do not employ some of them to produce American brands of software, they will not remain competitive.

3. For a strident but challenging argument that China's military does present a real threat, see Ross H. Munro, "Awakening Dragon: The Real Danger in Asia Is from China," *Policy Review*, Fall 1992. For a less alarming view of China's rising power, see Barber Conable and M. David Lampton, "China: The Coming Power," *Foreign Affairs*, Winter 1992.

4. According to some Chinese sources, China's military buildup is aimed at Taiwan, with plans already drawn up for an immediate invasion of Taiwan when it declares independence. A more likely scenario would involve various Chinese threats as Taiwan moved toward independence, ending with a possible attack if Taiwan persists.

5. Another mistaken belief in the United States is that China was on the verge of a democratic transition in 1989; one need only recall the numerous predictions after June 4 that the system was about to collapse. Even now there is no real opposition force in China that could step in and govern. Today many Chinese look back with some relief that the students did not take power in 1989.

2

Renewing China's Most-Favored-Nation Status Benefits Both Nations

Bill Clinton

Bill Clinton was elected the forty-second president of the United States in 1992.

It is in the best interest of America to renew China's most-favored-nation (MFN) trade status without the condition of human rights progress in China. But human rights abuses by China's government continue, and America will remain a champion of civil liberties in that nation. Renewing MFN will avoid isolating China from America and will allow both nations to pursue cultural, economic, educational, and other contacts. This increased engagement will be the most effective way to advance the cause of human rights in China.

Our relationship with China is important to all Americans. We have significant interests in what happens there and what happens between us. China has an atomic arsenal and a vote and a veto in the UN Security Council. It is a major factor in Asian and global security. We share important interests, such as in a nuclear-free Korean Peninsula and in sustaining the global environment. China is also the world's fastest-growing economy. Over $8 billion of U.S. exports to China in 1993 supported over 150,000 American jobs.

I have received Secretary Warren Christopher's letter, as required by 1993's executive order [Clinton in May 1993 ordered the extension of China's trade privileges with the United States], reporting to me on the conditions [outlined] in that executive order. He has reached a conclusion with which I agree: The Chinese did not achieve overall significant progress in all the areas outlined in the executive order relating to human rights, even though, clearly, there was progress made in important areas, including the resolution of all emigration cases, the establishment of a memorandum of understanding with regard to how prison labor issues

Bill Clinton, "U.S. Renews Most-Favored-Nation Trade Status for China," *U.S. Department of State Dispatch*, May 30, 1994.

would be resolved, the adherence to the Universal Declaration of Human Rights, and other issues. Nevertheless, serious human rights abuses continue in China, including the arrest and detention of those who peacefully voice their opinions and the repression of Tibet's religious and cultural traditions.

The question for us now is, given the fact that there has been some progress but that not all the requirements of the executive order were met, how can we best advance the cause of human rights and the other profound interests the United States has in its relationship with China?

Delinking human rights from MFN

I have decided that the United States should renew most-favored-nation trading status toward China. This decision, I believe, offers us the best opportunity to lay the basis for long-term sustainable progress in human rights and for the advancement of our other interests with China. Extending MFN will avoid isolating China and, instead, will permit us to engage the Chinese with not only economic contacts but with cultural, educational, and other contacts, and with a continuing aggressive effort in human rights—an approach that I believe will make it more likely that China will play a responsible role, both at home and abroad.

I am moving, therefore, to delink human rights from the annual extension of most-favored-nation trading status for China. That linkage has been constructive since May 1993. But I believe, based on our aggressive contacts with the Chinese, that we have reached the end of the usefulness of that policy, and it is time to take a new path toward the achievement of our constant objectives. We need to place our relationship into a larger and more productive framework.

In view of the continuing human rights abuses, I am extending the sanctions imposed by the United States as a result of the events in Tiananmen Square, and I am also banning the import of munitions, principally guns and ammunition, from China. I am also pursuing a new and vigorous American program to support those in China working to advance the cause of human rights and democracy.

I don't want to be misunderstood about this: China continues to commit very serious human rights abuses.

This program will include increased broadcasts for Radio Free Asia and the Voice of America, increased support for non-governmental organizations working on human rights in China, and the development with American business leaders of a voluntary set of principles for business activity in China. I don't want to be misunderstood about this: China continues to commit very serious human rights abuses. Even as we engage the Chinese on military, political, and economic issues, we intend to stay engaged with those in China who suffer from human rights abuses. The United States must remain a champion of their liberties.

I believe the question, therefore, is not whether we continue to support human rights in China, but how we can best support human rights in China and advance our other very significant issues and interests. I believe we can do it by engaging the Chinese. I believe the course I have chosen gives us the best chance of success on all fronts. We will have more contacts. We will have more trade. We will have more international cooperation. We will have more intense and constant dialogue on human rights issues. We will have that in an atmosphere which gives us the chance to see China evolve as a responsible power, ever-growing not only economically but growing in political maturity so that human rights can be observed.

To those who argue that in view of China's human rights abuses we should revoke MFN status, let me ask you the same question that I have asked myself over and over as I have studied this issue and consulted people of both parties who have had experience with China over many decades. Will we do more to advance the cause of human rights if China is isolated or if our nations are engaged in a growing web of political and economic cooperation and contacts? I am persuaded that the best path for advancing freedom in China is for the United States to intensify and broaden its engagement with that nation.

I think we have to see our relations with China within the broader context of our policies in the Asia-Pacific region, a region that, after all, includes our own nation. We've seen encouraging developments in 1994: progress on resolving trade frictions with the Japanese and possible progress toward stopping North Korea's nuclear program.

I am determined to see that we maintain an active role in this region, in both its dynamic economic growth and in its security. In three decades and three wars during this century, Americans have fought and died in the Asia-Pacific to advance our ideals and our security. Our destiny demands that we continue to play an active role in this region. The actions I have taken today to advance our security, to advance our prosperity, to advance our ideals, I believe, are the important and appropriate ones. I believe, in other words, this is in the strategic, economic, and political interests of both the United States and China. I am confident that over the long run this decision will prove to be the correct one.

3

America Should Maintain Most-Favored-Nation Status for a Stronger China

Bryce Harland

Bryce Harland was New Zealand's first ambassador to China and later its permanent representative to the United Nations.

China faces numerous threats to its stability, including an approaching change of leadership, a weakening of its central authority, and rising expectations among the young. These forces could culminate in a collapse of China's communist regime, resulting in economic and social turmoil that could spread to neighboring countries. By maintaining China's most-favored-nation trade status, America can help ensure the nation's stability and contribute to its economic and political progress.

After the Asia-Pacific Economic Cooperation summit in Seattle in November 1993, President Bill Clinton said "we've agreed . . . that the Asian-Pacific region should be a united one, not divided." He spoke of a "shared commitment to mutually beneficial cooperation." Those goals can hardly be achieved without good relations between the United States and China, a growing economic powerhouse and the most populous country in the world.

Clinton is seeking a constructive engagement with Chinese leaders. At Seattle he had a frank discussion with his Chinese counterpart, President Jiang Zemin. Neither gave much ground. Clinton warned Jiang that an extension of China's most-favored-nation (MFN) status would be contingent on satisfactory progress on a range of issues including human rights, weapons proliferation, and trade. Jiang rejected any attempt at interference in China's internal affairs and especially the attachment of conditions to MFN extension. There did not seem to be much common ground. The gap between the positions of the two leaders looked so wide that an outsider wondered whether it could be bridged before June 1994,

Bryce Harland, "For a Strong China." Reprinted with permission from *Foreign Policy* 94 (Spring 1994). Copyright 1994 by the Carnegie Endowment for International Peace.

when the MFN question has to be decided again. [MFN status was renewed in 1994 and 1995.]

There are reasons to hope that this gap can be closed. China now relies heavily on the American market to absorb the products of its burgeoning light industries and to maintain its high annual economic growth. The Chinese have already made some concessions and are apparently preparing to make more—notably on Red Cross access to political prisoners. [China suspended negotiations on access in 1994.] They may go further, as long as they are not seen to be doing so under pressure.

On the U.S. side, businesses are pressing for continued access to China as they realize that its enormous, growing market is one they cannot afford to leave to their competitors. Human rights organizations say they are not seeking to limit trade. They are putting emphasis more on specific objectives like access to prisoners than on larger issues like democracy. Those factors suggest more flexibility in the positions of the two sides than is immediately apparent.

Concern about future relations

But there are still grounds for concern about the future course of relations between America and China. The collapse of the Soviet Union has removed the main threat to the security of the United States and freed it to pursue its other interests more vigorously. Some Americans seem to doubt whether the United States needs Asian friends as much as it did during the Cold War. The Tiananmen Square incident, which took place in 1989, still strongly influences American attitudes toward China, even if the hostility is gradually diminishing. The annual MFN renewal process brings that lingering hostility to bear on the trade issue, coloring the debate about China in the media and in Congress. The debate cannot be limited to the questions mentioned specifically in Clinton's executive order of May 1993 [renewing MFN with a proviso of human rights improvement, which was removed one year later]. Other issues will be raised and will affect the result. Chinese nuclear tests, arms sales, and arms purchases are well publicized, especially when policy decisions are coming up in Washington, and are often presented as evidence of irresponsibility, if not deliberate mischief-making, by China.

There are still grounds for concern about the future course of relations between America and China.

Some analysts extrapolate China's present economic growth rate into the future, without much consideration of political uncertainties, and use it to support their view that China is on the way to becoming a threat to the United States. But is China likely to become so powerful that it could afford to take on the one remaining superpower? There seems little justification for that view. China has an enormous population, even in relation to its resources. For all its remarkable growth in recent years, it remains a poor country. And its economic prospects depend heavily on continued access to the American market. The Chinese are hardly in a position to go on the rampage. That is not to say that China has no expansionist urges—

of what powerful country could that be said? The practical question is whether China is, or is likely to become, strong enough to exert undue influence over other countries. Does it have the power to expand?

China's current problems make it doubtful that it does or will have that power. China is facing a change of leadership. The succession is a difficult time because in China leadership tends to be personal, rather than institutional. This time it is further complicated by the fact that the regime now bases its claim to legitimacy on economic success rather than on ideology. The decentralization essential for that success is weakening the central authority, especially over the fast-growing areas along the coast. As a result, it is becoming harder for Beijing to keep Guangzhou and Shanghai under control. Economic growth, together with the advent of international television, has generated rising expectations, especially among the young, that will be hard to meet with China's population and resources. The stability and unity of China are likely to be severely tested during the next few years. It is an open question whether [ailing leader] Deng Xiaoping's successor, whoever he is, will be able to hold the leadership together and maintain its authority throughout the country.

What does it matter, some observers ask, if the communist regime collapses and China falls into turmoil, as it did after the Manchu empire collapsed in 1911? They wonder whether it would be better if the coastal provinces could free themselves to join the rest of the Pacific rim in export-led growth. Better for whom? Inland China is presently benefiting from the growth on the coast and would not readily accept a breakup. Unlike the republics of the former Soviet Union, China's provinces, though distinct, are not easily separated because they are interdependent. The cost of disintegration would be high, and not just in economic terms. It would almost certainly mean disorder and strife, with much human suffering. China's neighbors, including Hong Kong, Taiwan, Vietnam, and Korea, would inevitably become involved and be forced to share the costs of disintegration. And it might not stop there. The war that engulfed the Pacific from 1941 to 1945 arose from disagreements between Japan and the United States over a weak and divided China. A similar collapse in the 1990s would shatter Clinton's goal of an Asia-Pacific region that is united, not divided.

If China comes through the tests that lie ahead united and strong, it may create problems for other countries. That is true of most great powers. But what happened earlier this century suggests that a weak and divided China would cause far greater problems than a strong one. China could once again become an object of international competition and stimulate rivalries that would make regional cooperation an idle dream.

American interests

When formulating its policies, the Clinton administration must take full account of the views of Congress and of ordinary Americans. They expect Clinton to demand greater observance of human rights, respect for world order, and fair play for American business. But the administration must take a broad view of America's interests and bear in mind its own long-term objectives.

The policies Deng Xiaoping began to introduce in 1978 are transforming China. It is still a poor and heavily populated country with a culture that has resisted foreign values. But by opening it up and introducing a market economy, Deng has launched a process of dynamic growth. The changes he inspired have raised the standard of living and given the Chinese people more freedom. They are not as free as people in Western countries, and some still suffer for their opinions. But ordinary Chinese citizens no longer live in constant fear, as they did under Mao Tse-tung [Chinese leader, 1949–1976]. They are more willing to speak openly, even with foreigners, and they do. That is the biggest change in China since the 1970s, and the one most fraught with implications for the future.

If the United States were to withdraw China's MFN status, China's income would fall sharply and the expansion of its market would slow dramatically. The people most directly affected would be those in China producing for the U.S. market and those in America exporting to China. But the damaging effects would not stop there. The withdrawal of MFN status would undermine support for the reform process and jeopardize all that has been achieved, in the political as well as the economic spheres. Far from advancing the cause of human rights, it could prejudice that cause severely.

To an outside observer, the interest of the United States seems to be in encouraging the process of economic and political change in China, not in disrupting it. The "mutually beneficial cooperation" Clinton spoke of in Seattle requires stability and continuity. To provide American business with market growth and American workers with new jobs, China must remain united and peaceful. It must be able to sell its products in America without fear of arbitrary interruption. China can help ease America's current economic problems through shared growth, provided it has continuing access to the American market.

Anyone who lived through the long confrontation between America and China, from 1950 to 1971, must share Clinton's hope for an Asia-Pacific region that is united, not divided. To achieve the relationship with China essential for that purpose, Americans will need perspective, as well as a vision for the future.

4

U.S. Policy Should Stress Trade with China

Robert Kapp

Robert Kapp is the president of the U.S.-China Business Council, a business and lobbying group in Washington, D.C.

America's policy should stress more engagement with China—especially increased trade and economic investment. Neither of these is likely if the United States ceases or restricts its trade relationship with China. If America rescinded China's most-favored-nation trade status, it would lose exports to China and weaken its leverage on human rights.

What should the United States do to China economically in order to compel its government to do what we demand of it politically? That is what we have been debating. How far should we go in turning the economic screws in order to engender political responses in China that we demanded of them? We will never get to the end of it.

The proper question that we should be asking is: Under what circumstances is China most likely to evolve, politically and socially, as well as economically, in directions most compatible with deeply cherished American values?

Every American is entitled to his hopes or her hopes for what China might become, as every Chinese is entitled to the same hopes for the United States, and there are things, of course, to hope for here, too. That is the question we should be asking, and on which we should be making policy. Under what circumstances will China go in directions that most Americans who hold to deeply cherished American values would find the most compatible and the most congenial?

If we ask that question, the obvious answer is, more engagement; more trade; more investment; more economic improvement within China through the engagement with the United States and the rest of the world economically; more educational and social interactions on top of the immense range which already have been developed in the last fifteen years; more cooperation on Asian-Pacific economic affairs à la APEC

Robert Kapp, Congressional testimony before the U.S. Senate Committee on Foreign Relations, Subcommittee on East Asian and Pacific Affairs, *U.S. Policy Toward China*, 103 Cong. 2nd sess., 4 May 1994, 723.

[Asia-Pacific Economic Cooperation summit], which was my life work in 1993 in Seattle; and more and closer cooperation in regional and global security and environmental issues. None of that is likely if the United States were to abrogate or degrade the trade relationship which is based on the 1980 trade agreement calling for reciprocal granting of MFN [most-favored-nation trade status; renewed for China in 1994 and 1995].

It is my sense that the two governments are in fact confronting a very serious policy failure far deeper and more ominous than the relatively confined question of maintaining normal trade relations. Degrading normal MFN-based trade will not be a U.S. victory; it will be a U.S. defeat.

[Bill Clinton's original] policy was based on the assumption that the threat of MFN revocation, not the revocation itself, would compel changes in China's domestic political conduct. There is no alternative to MFN, blunt instrument though it be, as a way of making, or, if you will, inducing the Chinese to change certain aspects of their practices.

It is strongly likely that the degrading of the U.S. MFN relationship with China would induce Chinese retaliations.

But we are now at the point where we either have to fish or cut bait. Everybody can understand that the minute that MFN goes down the leverage on human rights that we thought we had is completely gone.

So the policy of the last few years that emphasized that it would be the threat that made the difference has reached the point of no return, the point of nullity.

The fact [is] that unilateral sanctions are compromised from the start. We simply have to recognize that degrading the trade relationship between the United States and China would itself be compromised if other countries did not play, and we all, I think, understand that they will not play.

Unlike the NAFTA [North American Free Trade Agreement], in which [opposing] sides could haul out or hire an economist and argue that jobs would be gained or jobs would be lost and we could never really prove it—unlike NAFTA, it is strongly likely that the degrading of the U.S. MFN relationship with China would induce Chinese retaliations, and the job loss from those retaliations would be specific and traceable.

On the day when we close the market to them, and perhaps they return the favor, the clear relationship to loss of employment in the United States will not be in doubt. In short, we look policy failure in the face, and the momentary glow of, if you will, righteousness when we take a very serious step in this regard would not be the last feeling that the United States had on the subject of the wisdom of the policy.

Let me go on and deal with several of the points which enter the discussion of the MFN debate in Congress and elsewhere in the public dialogue.

Number one, trade versus human rights is a completely false dichotomy. It has no validity. It is a headline writer's and subheadline writer's tool in little indented heads and articles, but in fact "trade vs. human rights" is a false dichotomy that legislators and policymakers should simply reject once and for all.

[Number two,] the implication that U.S. business with China is responsible for inadequacies in China's human rights record is not only without basis, it does little credit to those who casually employ the slogan. Similarly, the suggestion that U.S. business is "bankrolling China's dictators." . . . We denounce the Chinese for sloganeering in their politics, but the notion that U.S. business is bankrolling Chinese dictatorship, or Beijing's dictators, falls into the same category. We should get out of that business as well.

Number three, the familiar dialogue about the "butchers of Beijing." This language may be great in certain political contexts, but it is incompatible with sound policymaking on an issue of such importance to the U.S. national interest.

I might say that regarding the happy agreement between [Palestine Liberation Organization chairman] Yasser Arafat and [Israeli] prime minister Rabin relating to the Gaza [Strip] and to Jericho, a reporter noted that as the document was signed, 5,000 [Palestinians] were released from jail as the Israelis had pledged to do, but that human rights sources said that there were at least 10,000 in custody altogether. Not a peep from the U.S. government about these detentions.

So I think this rhetoric of the butchers of Beijing and the kind of focusing in some ways very selectively on issues in China is not entirely, shall I say, honest.

Imports and exports

Let me turn to one more that comes up a lot: we sell 2 percent of our exports to them, they sell 40 percent to us, therefore they need us so much that if we hold the line they will give in.

The first thing to say is, if you kill MFN, you can say goodbye to 3 percent of our exports going to China, or 4 or 5 or 10, which is a very serious thing to think about. Two percent may not be a lot. It is a lot in dollar terms, and it is a lot to those who are making the products, but it is small compared to perhaps 5 or 8 percent of U.S. exports. All of that is out of the picture if we turn off the spigot of MFN.

The other point, of course, about Chinese exports to the United States is that a lot of their product coming in now is coming in from factories placed on the mainland [by] Hong Kong and Taiwan, with Hong Kong and Taiwan capital. The overall trade deficit, if you will, between the United States and these three entities taken together is not that different than it was before.

Let me just say that in our [U.S.-China Business Council] view the time has come for the president really to lead, and to lead, he should in fact come out and say that we are on the wrong track, we are asking the wrong question, that the greatest interest for the United States as a nation and for our hopes for human rights improvements in China lies in full engagement, including the maximum economic engagement that we can develop with the People's Republic, and he should simply move us into this new track. That is true leadership.

The political packages—that is, the targeted sanctions, the raising [of tariffs by] 10 percent to see whether or not they gave—these will not score political points for the administration, in my view.

He needs to lead. My hope is that when he does lead, thinking Members of Congress, both parties, both Houses, will have made it clear, quietly or, perhaps, publicly that when he leads they will welcome his leadership and stay with him in embarking on a new and more realistic and successful engagement with China, including in this realistic and successful engagement a greater likelihood of real progress and real overall long-term progress in the improvement of what we consider to be the most necessary human rights conditions in the People's Republic of China.

There is room for presidential leadership. There is room, great room for congressional statesmanship.

5

U.S. Policy Should Not Link Trade to Chinese Human Rights Protection

James Finn

James Finn is the senior editor of the bimonthly magazine Freedom Review, *published by Freedom House, an organization that promotes freedom worldwide. He is also the chairman of Puebla Institute, a lay Catholic human rights organization in Washington, D.C.*

The U.S. government's threat to make China's most-favored-nation trade status conditional on improved human rights conditions within that country has been ineffective. Rather than threatening sanctions, the United States should increase trade with China. Increased trade would improve human rights by contributing to the creation of a middle class and by introducing new information and technology into Chinese society.

If foreign policies had a death wish, the U.S. policy on China enunciated in May 1993 could be said to have fulfilled it. It seemed designed to founder. China gained Most Favored Nation (MFN) trade status under President Jimmy Carter. This MFN status, which has been subsequently renewed through the Reagan and Bush administrations, was threatened when President Bill Clinton turned a campaign promise into an executive order that linked its further extension to "overall, significant progress" on human rights in China. No such improvement, no MFN. The State Department's evaluation of such progress, or the lack of it, is scheduled to land on the president's desk on June 3, 1994, a date that also marks the fifth anniversary of the massacre of Tiananmen Square. [In May 1994 Clinton renewed China's MFN status and reversed his policy of linking such renewal to human rights progress by China's government.] The administration shows uneasiness about the corner into which it has boxed itself. For if the policy has the advantage of being clear-cut and unqualified, it also has the concomitant disadvantages.

The Clinton administration is being forced to look more closely at

James Finn, "How Not to Punish China," *Commonweal*, May 20, 1994; ©1994 Commonweal Foundation. Reprinted with permission.

some home truths. China now has the third largest and the fastest-growing economy in the world. In 1993 it exported $33 billion worth of goods to the United States from which it imported about $9 billion worth, for a very favorable surplus. This trade involves a significant number of workers on both sides of the trade balance, and further billions in future contracts. A serious rupture in this trade—the withdrawal of MFN status and the imposition of broad sanctions—would cause severe losses for both Chinese and American interests, although China could look to other trading partners.

The policy declared in the executive order was intended to use these interests as a lever to force China to improve its human rights practices, its handling of political prisoners, its relations with Tibet, and its disruption of foreign news broadcasts. When Warren Christopher made his much publicized trip to China in March 1994, he stated these concerns directly to his hosts. Even more bluntly, his hosts told the secretary of state they did not welcome his intrusions into their internal affairs and that the importance of trade between the two countries had been overstated. (Foreign Minister Qian Qiche later said that during the twenty-three years in which there was no trade between China and the United States, "I think you lived quite well. And so did we.") To add to this sharp rebuff, the Chinese authorities harassed dissidents on the occasion of Christopher's visit. Part bluff, part traditional sensitivity to foreign influences, but not beyond anticipation.

Disregard for human rights

China's clear lack of interest in displaying improvement in its human rights practices is confirmed by organizations such as Asia Watch and Puebla Institute, which have documented specific human rights abuses and particular people who have suffered them. The latter organization has reported that, in fact, "repression of Christians by the Chinese government increased significantly since mid-1993." (In the interest of full disclosure: I am chairman of Puebla.) Given this record there can be no fair finding that China has made overall significant progress in human rights during the subsequent year.

On the basis of these facts, many commentators as well as policymakers have described the situation as a head-on conflict between expediency and principles, between commercial and moral interests. In fact, the Clinton policy seems to set up that very confrontation—which is why the policymakers are unhappy and why the policy is inadequate to the reality.

Some of the factors that have been left out of the equation include the real interests of other Asian countries, including U.S. allies; the role of China in cooperative political ventures with the United States; the effect of further market economy inroads in China; and the effect of a prospering, peaceful China in Asia.

No Asian country supports the U.S. policy linking MFN and human rights improvement in China. This is partly because they do not give human rights as much weight in formulating foreign policy as does the United States, but also because they fear the possible consequences of a U.S.-China confrontation. This fear is measured not only in economic terms—trade, money, and jobs, all of which depend on a prospering

China—but in terms of the Asian balance of power, stability, and chances of long-range peace. The United States has an important role to play if these goals are to be achieved, a role that would be grievously impaired by a Sino-American conflict. North Korea may prove intransigent in its refusal to allow proper oversight of its nuclear facilities, but there is a better chance of changing its present stance if China and the United States cooperate in the effort.

Perhaps the most important factor, however, is the deleterious effect extensive sanctions would have on the Chinese people themselves—the people, not the government. One of Karl Marx's most penetrating insights is pertinent here: "The bourgeosie, by the rapid improvement of all instruments of production, by the immensely facilitated means of communication, draws all, even the most backward, nations into civilization . . . it batters down all Chinese walls...it forces the underdeveloped nations' intensely obstinate hatred of foreigners to capitulate."

Trade helps human rights

One of the most effective ways to improve the condition of human rights in China is to increase, not diminish, trade with China. Improvement within China during the last ten or twelve years supports this judgment. Not only does such trade help produce a middle class, with increasingly sophisticated political and social views, but it introduces new information and values into an insular society. Tiananmen Square remains a great blot on China's record, but it is well to note that the world would have known little of that event if advanced communication technology had not transmitted it almost instantly to every corner of the globe. China's subsequent denials fell on informed ears that knew better. Increased trade means an increase in high-tech communications both in China and between China and other countries. It is a potent lever to open that society to outside values.

> *One of the most effective ways to improve the condition of human rights in China is to increase, not diminish, trade with China.*

Anyone still skeptical about the transforming effect of modern communications should consider the last years and days of the Soviet Union. In early 1991, before the failed coup attempt of August, independent Soviet coal miners initiated a series of strikes across the country. They spoke in the name of democracy and reform in a voice that could not be entirely ignored. They were able to do this because the AFL-CIO [American Federation of Labor and Congress of Industrial Organizations] in this country had but recently helped them procure computers, faxes, modems, etc. This technology allowed groups of miners who were united in spirit but separated by vast distance to do what was previously impossible, to communicate rapidly and coordinate their activities. As one of the most powerful forces fighting for democracy, they helped defeat the coup planned by the State Committee for the State of Emergency and paved the way for the election of Boris Yeltsin as president. Without the efforts of the workers' movement—made possible only by rapid internal communication—it is doubtful that this transforming event in Soviet/Russian history would have developed as it did.

For these reasons, the linkage between MFN and a marked improvement in human rights should be broken. The United States should not force itself to choose between drastically reducing trade with China, on the one hand, and on the other, justifying continued MFN status by devising the most transparent fig-leaf of supposed improvement in its human rights record. This most emphatically does not mean dislodging considerations of human rights from U.S. interests and policies. That plank should be firmly in place. Violations of human rights should be disclosed and condemned in various forums. Pressure for reform should come from both governmental and nongovernmental agencies. The work of organizations such as Asia Watch and Puebla deserves strong support and encouragement. But their efforts should not be made to contest with other desirable, even necessary, policies.

6

U.S.-Chinese Cooperation Strengthens Asia-Pacific Security

William Perry

William Perry was appointed U.S. secretary of defense in February 1994. Perry served in the Pentagon during the Jimmy Carter administration as undersecretary for research and engineering and is credited with ushering in the development of stealth technology and cruise missiles. The following is from a speech delivered at the National Defense University in Beijing, China, on October 18, 1994.

East Asia is more peaceful and stable now than at any time in the past. Its gross domestic product compares to that of America and Europe combined. The United States and China share a special responsibility to ensure the region's stability and prosperity. Several regional security challenges involving the Korean Peninsula, South Asia, the South China Sea, and Taiwan require U.S.-Chinese cooperation, including strong military ties.

British author Graham Greene once wrote that "There always comes a moment in time when a door opens and lets the future in." With the ending of the Cold War, a door has opened for the Asia-Pacific region. Together, the nations of this region can work to shape that future to make it prosperous, peaceful, and secure.

The Asia-Pacific region today is more peaceful and more stable than at any time in its history. The rivalry of the Cold War has been washed away by a flood tide of democracy and economic progress. And throughout the region, there is a sense of increased confidence and optimism about the future. The seeds of this triumph were actually sown during the Cold War as Asian nations undertook market reforms and began building strong trade links with their neighbors and the rest of the world. The results have been extraordinary.

The gross domestic product of this region essentially matches that of the United States and Europe combined. Asia now accounts for one-third

William Perry, "The Sino-U.S. Relationship and Its Impact on World Peace," *U.S. Department of State Dispatch*, October 31, 1994.

of the world's gross world product. This enormous economic growth now makes the prosperity of Asia essential to the economic health of the world. And good economic relations require healthy political ties. Consequently, leaders around the globe are placing increased importance on their relations with the nations of this region. President Clinton has done so, including convening the first-ever meeting of leaders of the region in November 1993 in Seattle, at which time he met [Chinese] president Jiang Zemin.

The challenge facing us today is to ensure that this region's stability and prosperity are strengthened for future generations. The United States and China share a special responsibility for making this happen. I want to talk about the reasons why our security relationship is so important and about some of the most important challenges that we face. I want to talk about the importance of building ties between our two militaries.

The importance of stability

There are four principal reasons why the United States and China share a special responsibility to secure the present and future stability in the West Pacific.

The first is strategic. The size of our countries and their populations, our vast natural resources, and the creative spirit of our peoples combine to make the United States and China key players in the Asia-Pacific region, with China at one end of the Pacific and the United States at the other. Together, we play a defining role in every aspect of the region's economy and security. This is not an idle boast. I do not want to downplay the contributions of other nations in the region, but history shows that when the United States and China enjoy positive, stable relations, the entire region benefits.

The second reason our nations have a special obligation to get along is that we have many overlapping interests. Both the United States and China regard economic progress and the economic well-being of our people as a vital national priority. Economic progress requires, above all, stability and peace. Fortunately, the economic strengths of our two countries complement each other, and the forces favoring cooperation between us are growing stronger all the time.

The third reason our relationship is so important is the danger posed by proliferation of weapons of mass destruction and their delivery systems. China and the United States are two of a handful of nations capable of producing both. In October 1994, our two governments signed important agreements to control missile transfers and fissile material production. This was an important step, but more needs to be done to promote global security by limiting weapons of terror and mass destruction.

Restraint by China in transferring these technologies, in concert with the United States and other major powers, is vital to the success of current, global non-proliferation regimes. Indeed, without the full participation of both China and the United States, no effort against proliferation can be successful.

Fourth, because China and the United States play such key roles in Asia, our cooperation is essential to solving the major threats to regional stability. This won't be easy. The Cold War world was one of great danger, but it was also somewhat stable. The thaw that came with the end of the Cold War alleviated one of the greatest dangers—that of a nuclear world war. But the new world is more complex—and still dangerous. Right now, Asia faces many challenges and threats to its stability—challenges and threats that require Chinese-American cooperation. I want to focus on four of those challenges.

Regional security challenges

First, the most serious challenge is on the Korean Peninsula There is both a nuclear and a political connection to this challenge.

Let me consider first the nuclear dimension. If North Korea produces nuclear weapons, the peace and security of Northeast Asia will be threatened, and the worldwide effort to control weapons of mass destruction will be dealt a heavy blow. I have discussed this with Minister of National Defense Chi, and I believe that we have a common view on this issue. North Korea must honor its commitment to the Non-Proliferation Treaty and to its agreement with South Korea for a denuclearized Korean Peninsula.

Both the United States and China support a nuclear-free Korean Peninsula. In 1994, we were deeply engaged in discussions and dialogue with North Korea. These negotiations in Geneva reached agreement. I am hopeful that this agreement will result in the ending of the nuclear threat from North Korea. All during these negotiations, we consulted very closely with your government, which has been very helpful.

The second dimension of this challenge is finding ways to reduce the overall tensions on the peninsula that have plagued the Korean people and their neighbors for half a century. We are deeply interested in the long-term future of the Korean Peninsula and its contribution to peace and stability in the region. And we want to work with China to ensure that peace and stability. But only the Korean people themselves can address the root causes of the tensions between them. That is why it is so important for the North and South to revive their dialogue and work toward removing military confrontation and increasing economic and human ties.

The challenge facing us today is to ensure that [the Asia-Pacific] region's stability and prosperity are strengthened.

Reducing tensions in Northeast Asia also depends on other outside factors. America's security alliances and military presence in Northeast Asia, I believe, are key components of the region's stability. A keystone of security in Asia is the firm fabric of strategic ties and the military alliance between the United States and Japan. The people and the governments of Japan and the United States are committed to maintaining and strengthening the alliance to deal with the challenges of the post–Cold War world. I believe that this alliance is a force for stability.

The American and South Korean security alliance is also an important force for regional peace and stability. The United States will maintain a ground and air military presence on the peninsula for as long as the Republic of Korea and the Korean people feel that it meets their security interests.

The second challenge to regional security in Asia lies in South Asia. We are on the brink of a nuclear weapons race on the subcontinent, where relations between India and Pakistan have been tense for years. India and Pakistan both have the right to a strong defense, but the combination of nuclear weapons and enduring tension could prove catastrophic to both countries—indeed, to the entire region. As in the case with Korea, China has a huge stake in this issue since it involves nations on its borders.

With so much at stake, it is essential that countries with influence in South Asia try to stop the potential arms race before it gathers momentum. The recent progress between the United States and China on missile technology and fissile material is a positive step in that direction. But we must do more if we are to prevent a South Asia nuclear arms race.

A third challenge we face lies in the South China Sea. This situation has been a source of tension for years, and it creates anxiety about the future. If disputed territorial claims to the Spratly Islands erupt into conflict, it could be a devastating blow to regional security and could threaten sea lines of communication vital to the United States and other countries of the world. Inflammatory statements and military deployments help keep tensions high. They also prevent the development of natural resources which might help reduce tensions. That is why I am encouraged by the stated desire of China and Vietnam to avoid conflict. I am also encouraged by the Indonesian-led efforts to find a long-term solution to the disputed territorial claims involving other nations. What is needed are permanent and peaceful solutions to these problems.

The fourth regional security issue is Taiwan. Since 1972, six American administrations have demonstrated America's commitment to abide by the terms of the Taiwan Relations Act and the three communiques between China and the United States. Responsibility for resolving differences lies with Chinese on both sides of the Taiwan Straits. The overriding United States interest is that the resolution be peaceful and not threaten regional security. Not long ago, relations across the straits reflected fierce hostility between the two sides. But, today, economic and cultural relations are robust and growing stronger every day.

More significantly, political contacts appear to be developing at a pace with which both sides are comfortable. We welcome any progress that the two sides can agree upon. Overall, military tension has been reduced and the situation is far less volatile.

This is a promising trend accomplished by the two sides. And we believe that our policies contributed to these positive developments. These policies include strict adherence to the agreements between China and the United States and include the maintenance of unofficial relations with Taiwan. This will not change.

U.S.-China cooperation

None of the challenges to Asian stability and security can be fully met without cooperation between the United States and China. Each of us has a particular kind of influence and each of us must use this influence appropriately. Maintaining regional stability is our cooperative task. It is also the strategic basis for our relationship.

An important component of a healthy political relationship between our two countries is military-to-military ties. By building trust, these ties contribute to our ability to solve regional problems.

One way that military ties build trust is by helping both sides understand each other's defense policies and strategic intentions. Both of our countries need to do better in this area. China is a large country with a proud, independent spirit. Your capabilities in all areas, including military areas, are growing every day. This growth, particularly in the military area, creates much speculation in Washington and in capitals throughout Asia.

> *None of the challenges to Asian stability and security can be fully met without cooperation between the United States and China.*

We welcome your assurances about the focus of your defense budget and the peaceful, defensive orientation of your modernization program. Nevertheless, it would be helpful if your defense budget and strategic planning were more open and visible to the outside world. This would contribute to stability in the Asia-Pacific region. We have nothing to fear from a better understanding of each other.

Of course, we understand that this is a two-way street. We want you to know about U.S. military planning as well. I know that some in China believe that the United States regards China as a threat or, at least, a future threat.

As secretary of defense of the United States, I can assure you that those who make these arguments do not understand American defense policy. The fact that some people believe them just highlights the need for greater openness and understanding.

For all of these reasons, I am pleased that we have begun rebuilding ties between our militaries. In August 1994, your deputy chief of general staff, General Xu Huizi, visited the United States. We were able to talk very frankly and productively about each other's concerns. I am convinced that our two militaries are working toward the same goals of mutual understanding, peace, and stability.

We want to build military-to-military ties with China that will endure long into the future. Doing this means building a consensus and a strong foundation of domestic support in the United States. No military relationship can grow in a vacuum, and it cannot survive without a healthy political relationship.

I must tell you that the idea of U.S.-China military-to-military ties has its critics in the United States, in the capitals of our allies, and, I'm sure, in China as well. That's why we must proceed cautiously and within a framework of overall progress in our relations, including difficult issues such as nonproliferation and human rights. But we must proceed.

I envision a relationship that is led by our defense officials but which rests on a solid foundation of officers—like yourselves—who will lead the armed forces into the twenty-first century. I can assure you that your American counterparts, who also proudly wear their uniform, share this vision.

In the past 200 years, the United States and China have met under various circumstances and for various purposes. At times, we have opposed each other; at other times, we've been drawn together by common interests.

From the outset of his Administration, President Clinton decided that our countries needed to follow the path of cooperation instead of confrontation. That is why he launched a policy of comprehensive engagement, including a resumption of military ties. And that is why he renewed most-favored-nation trading status for China—to pave the way for expanding our ties. I have strongly supported these policies. Now the challenge is to use our expanded ties for our mutual advantage and for the benefit of peoples around the world.

China is a great nation. China's influence reaches every corner of Asia and, increasingly, the world. Your future is important to us and to all of the Asia-Pacific region—indeed, is important to the world.

In the Chinese classic *The Art of War* by Sun Tzu, there is some good advice about how to maintain peace. It says,

> Always remember danger when you are secure and remember chaos in times of order, watch out for danger and chaos while they are still formless and prevent them before they happen.

I hope my trip to China helps both our nations use the security and order in our present relationship to prevent dangers and to build a lasting peace for the future.

7

America and China Should Cooperate to Protect Intellectual Property Rights

Wu Yi

Wu Yi is the minister of foreign trade for the People's Republic of China.

The Chinese government has formally committed to cracking down on violations of American intellectual property rights. It instructs prosecutors to actively pursue infringement cases and requires Chinese courts to address intellectual property rights cases expeditiously. U.S. government agencies can help China protect these rights by providing equipment, personnel, and training. Regular consultation and exchanges of intellectual property rights information between both countries will benefit enforcement and protection.

Editor's note: The following letter to U.S. trade representative Mickey Kantor dated February 26, 1995, was confirmed the same day by Kantor as an understanding between the United States and China.

I have the honor to refer to the consultations between representatives of the Government of the People's Republic of China (China) and the Government of the United States of America (United States) which were conducted in the spirit of the 1992 Memorandum of Understanding between our governments concerning the protection of intellectual property rights. Both of our governments are committed to providing adequate and effective protection and enforcement of intellectual property rights and have agreed to provide this to each other's nationals.

China's actions in this respect show considerable progress and determination to achieve effective enforcement of intellectual property rights through judicial and administrative procedures. China has created specialized intellectual property courts to hear these cases and I can confirm that the Civil and Criminal Procedure Laws of the People's Republic of

---

Wu Yi, letter to U.S. trade representative Mickey Kantor, February 26, 1995.

China empower the courts to address infringement of intellectual property rights through measures to stop infringement, preserve property before and during litigation, and to order the infringer to provide compensation to right owners for infringement of their intellectual property rights. In addition, the courts also act to preserve evidence to permit effective litigation.

China's Supreme People's Court has issued a circular instructing courts at various levels to address intellectual property cases expeditiously, including cases involving foreign right holders. In respect of taking criminal action against infringers, our procuratorates [sic] are actively pursuing criminal infringement cases.

An action plan

I have attached to this letter a State Council Intellectual Property Enforcement Action Plan [excluded from this viewpoint] that will be carried out immediately. This Action Plan strengthens the enforcement efforts that China has already taken and establishes a long-term enforcement structure so that the people's governments in the provinces, directly administered municipalities, autonomous regions and cities meet the requirements of that Plan and China will actively implement it. Under Chinese law, each administrative authority mentioned in the Action Plan is fully empowered to take the specified steps to effectively enforce intellectual property rights.

Chinese authorities have recently taken effective actions to enforce intellectual property rights. Recently, seven plans producing infringing products have been closed, business licenses revoked, and more than two million infringing CDs, LDs [laser discs] and copies of computer software have been seized and destroyed. Under the Chinese government's Action Plan, this effort will intensify and by July 1, 1995, investigation of all production lines suspected of producing infringing CDs, LDs and CD-ROMs [compact disc–read-only memory] will be completed. Factories that have engaged in infringing activities will be punished through seizure and forfeiture of infringing product and all infringing copies will be destroyed and the materials and implements directly and predominantly used to make the infringing product will be seized, forfeited and destroyed. Business licenses and permits will also continue to be revoked in appropriate cases.

China confirms that it will not impose quotas, import license requirements or other restrictions on the importation of audio-visual and published products.

Exports of infringing products have been banned. The establishment of a copyright verification system and the use of unique identifiers on CDs, CD-ROMs and LDs will provide a vital tool to prevent the production of infringing goods and export of those goods. Permits to engage in activities related to audio-visual products will not be issued without copyright verification and imprint of the unique identifier. More than one violation of this condition will result in revocation of the permit and repeat serious offenders will have their business licenses revoked.

Retail establishments will be inspected under the Action Plan and enterprises will keep records of inventories and other information to strengthen enforcement. Recent raids on computer software enterprises are an example of China's effective enforcement of intellectual property rights.

Another aspect of China's decision to develop its economy and open its markets further is increased cooperation and trade in products protected by intellectual property rights. China has recently approved the establishment of a representative office for the International Federation of Phonogram Industries (IFPI) and will examine and approve, when published requirements are met, the pending application of the relevant entity for the verification of motion picture copyrights, as well as other entities involved in copyright verification. Obtaining this approval does not prejudice the ability of these offices to engage in other activities in accord with Chinese laws and regulations.

Joint ventures

China confirms that it will not impose quotas, import license requirements or other restrictions on the importation of audio-visual and published products, whether formal or informal. China will permit U.S. individuals and entities to establish joint ventures with Chinese entities in China in the audio-visual sector for production and reproduction. These joint ventures will be permitted to enter into contracts with Chinese publishing enterprises to, on a nationwide basis, distribute, sell, display and perform in China. China will immediately permit such joint ventures to be established in Shanghai, Guangzhou and moreover, other major cities, and will then expand the number of these cities, in an orderly fashion, to thirteen by the year 2000. U.S. individuals and entities will be permitted to enter into exclusive licensing arrangements with Chinese publishing houses to exploit the entire catalogue of the licensor and to decide what to release from that catalogue. China will also permit U.S. individuals and entities to establish joint ventures in the computer software sector, and these joint ventures will be permitted to produce and sell computer software and computer software products in China.

China will continue to permit U.S. individuals and entities to enter into revenue sharing arrangements with Chinese entities. Permissible arrangements will include, for example, licensing agreements under which the U.S. entity receives a negotiated percentage of revenues generated by film products.

China will adopt or enforce measures necessary to protect public morals or to maintain public order, as long as such measures are applied consistently and in a non-discriminatory, non-arbitrary manner and do not operate as a disguised restriction on trade. By October 1, 1995, China will publish all laws, rules, regulations, administrative guidance, or other official documents concerning any limitation on, regulation of or permission required to engage in all activities identified above. The audio-visual departments under the State Council will intensify their efforts to formulate the regulatory rules on audio-visual products, which will clarify the specific censorship regulations for publication and importation of audio-visual products. For audio-visual products that meet the provisions of the censorship requirements, their publication and import will be approved without any restrictions in terms of quantity. The censorship regulations will be open, transparent and published. Determinations as to censorship requirements will normally be made within ten days, but in no event longer than sixty days from receipt of an application.

In light of China's policies of market opening, representatives of U.S. enterprises are invited to begin discussions on their establishment in China, including possible licensing arrangements, as soon as possible.

U.S. assistance

It is my understanding that the United States will provide assistance to China with respect to the protection and enforcement of intellectual property rights. This work will be implemented mainly through the U.S. Customs Service, U.S. Department of Justice and the United States Patent and Trademark Office.

The U.S. Customs Service is prepared to provide cooperative and reciprocal assistance to China on providing improved enforcement of intellectual property rights. This assistance and coordination effort could include: (1) providing training, in China, by U.S. Customs personnel of Chinese customs officers with responsibility for enforcing intellectual property rights; and (2) providing mutually agreed relevant technical equipment to assist in the enforcement of intellectual property rights. Training will likely include: how to identify infringing merchandise through physical examination, verification of documents, and laboratory testing, and assistance in building a centralized system of intellectual property rights recordations. The U.S. Patent and Trademark Office will also assist in training Chinese personnel, including through providing training and documents for the people who work on verification of well-known [trade]marks and mechanisms for establishing an administrative appeals process.

China and the United States will exchange information and statistics on a quarterly basis beginning on June 1, 1995, on intellectual property enforcement activities in their two countries. Beginning on January 1, 1996, this exchange will be carried out on a semi-annual basis for the next two years, and on a schedule to be agreed thereafter.

The United States will provide assistance to China with respect to the protection and enforcement of intellectual property rights.

Under these exchanges, China will provide information and statistics concerning enforcement, throughout the country, of intellectual property rights of U.S. nationals and joint ventures with U.S. nationals by type of intellectual property, establishments raided and the value and disposition of infringing products and machinery and implements. Information and statistics on prosecutions and administrative and court decisions will also be provided.

Under these exchanges, the United States will provide to China, on the same schedule, information and statistics concerning the customs seizure value of infringing goods by commodity, the seizure value of infringing goods by type of intellectual property right, the seizure value of Chinese infringing goods by commodity and the seizure quantities of infringing goods by commodity. The United States will also provide statistics on federal intellectual property enforcement activities, including information on prosecutions for copyright infringement and trademark counterfeiting and court decisions in intellectual property cases. The United States will also provide information and statistics on Chinese products that are infringed in the United States.

China and the United States will, upon request, consult and exchange information on the license verification system set out in the Action Plan and particular applications of that system. China and the United States require that public entities in both countries shall not use unauthorized copies of computer software in their computer systems and legitimate software will be used. They likewise require that adequate resources shall be provided to permit the acquisition only of authorized computer software.

In addition, China and the United States will consult promptly at the request of either government with respect to any matter affecting the operation or the implementation of the provisions of this letter, including its annex. In addition, both governments agree to consult, during the first year on a quarterly basis, semiannually for the following two years and then on a schedule to be agreed, on the implementation of the Action Plan and its effectiveness.

On the basis of the foregoing, the United States will immediately revoke China's designation as a "special 301" priority foreign country [under the 1974 Trade Act], and will terminate the section 301 investigation of China's enforcement of intellectual property rights and market access for persons who rely on intellectual property protection and rescind the order issued by the U.S. Trade Representative on February 4, 1995, imposing increased tariffs on Chinese exports.

Please confirm that this letter, including its annex, and your letter in reply constitute an Understanding between our two governments.

8

Bill Clinton Should Not Have Renewed China's Most-Favored-Nation Status

The Progressive

The monthly Progressive, *founded in 1909, is one of America's oldest politically liberal magazines.*

Bill Clinton displayed a lack of commitment to human rights protection by renewing China's most-favored-nation trade status in 1994. Clinton's policy is not designed to promote human rights in China, but to advance the interests of U.S. corporations. Particularly appalling is the green light his policy sends to human rights abusers worldwide. Political prisoners in many countries should not expect America's government to provide relief from oppression.

By renewing China's "most-favored-nation" status, president Bill Clinton has shown once and for all that in his Administration, human rights take a back seat to corporate profits. Despite his blushing remarks that China has made "some progress in important areas," Clinton could convince no rational person—not even himself—that China has taken significant steps since 1993 toward improving its sorry human-rights record. Under Clinton's own executive order, that should have meant the end of China's preferential trade treatment, but Clinton simply reversed course once again and conferred "most-favored-nation" status [without a link to human-rights progress] anyway. The only punitive measure he imposed was an insignificant ban on the import of made-in-China firearms and ammunition. Ouch!

One needed to look no further than the business pages to find out why Clinton caved. Clue: It was not to "advance our ideals," which was one of the reasons Clinton adduced for his policy. Instead, it was simply to advance the interests of U.S. corporations. The day after Clinton's announcement, U.S. companies were crowing. AT&T, McDonnell Douglas, Boeing, J.C. Penney, Sears, Kmart, and the Gap all applauded the deci-

"Coddler-in-Chief," *The Progressive*, July 1994. Reprinted by permission of *The Progressive*, 409 E. Main St., Madison, WI 53703.

sion. These companies either manufacture goods in China, sell goods to China, or import goods from China, and they would have lost a great deal if U.S. trade relations with China had gone sour.

The sums involved were not insignificant. Boeing, for example, was negotiating to sell China fifty commercial aircraft for $5 billion, and AT&T, according to the *New York Times*, "expects to collect $3 billion in revenue from its China operations by the year 2000."

Not surprisingly, the Chinese rulers also lauded the decision, having won their game of chicken with the Clinton Administration. "The Chinese Government and people welcome this decision of President Clinton," the foreign ministry declared, calling it a "historic opportunity" for improving relations between the two countries.

Human-rights abuses in Cuba pale in comparison to those in China. So why the continued embargo on Cuba alongside the clear sailing for China?

In the months leading up to Clinton's decision, the Chinese government not only arrested a number of leading dissidents, including Wei Jingsheng; it also arrogated to itself vast new powers of repression. Crimes are now on the books for "disturbing public order and damaging people's health through religious activities," for "stirring up conflicts between nationalities," and, most broadly, for "doing harm to the public interest," reports Lena Sun of the *Washington Post*. Reports of arrests, torture, and secret trials continue to pour in, Sun noted. The Chinese Government released a few political prisoners for show, but the overall record is clear and inescapable.

Secretary of State Warren Christopher said, "We're not backing away in any way from pursuing human-rights problems" in China. That may be the most blatant lie yet out of the Clinton Administration, though there is certainly a tight contest for that distinction.

In its essence, Clinton's policy is now no different from the one previously pursued by George Bush, which Clinton had savaged during the 1992 Presidential campaign. Clinton, remember, had said Bush was "coddling tyrants" in China. Clinton now is the Coddler-in-chief, and the only way to distinguish his policy from Bush's was to listen to the ritual calisthenic groaning Clinton emitted before doing the wrong thing.

Clinton's policy toward China is particularly appalling because of the green light it sends to other human-rights abusers around the globe: Their economic relations with the United States count for much more than their treatment of their own subjects. And to political prisoners in Burma, Indonesia, Guatemala, Colombia, Zaire, Egypt, Turkey, or anywhere in this troubled world, the signal is also clear: Don't look to Washington for relief from oppression.

To "delink" economic policy from human-rights policy, as Clinton announced, is a step backward into the Kissingerian [after former U.S. secretary of state Henry Kissinger] abyss. The crass cynicism of Clinton's bow to the commercial imperative (subhead in the *New York Times*: PROFIT MOTIVE GETS THE NOD) should revolt anyone who cares about human rights.

China and Cuba: a double standard

Clinton's rationale for keeping China's "most-favored-nation" trade status sheds a peculiar light on U.S. policy toward Cuba. Clinton concluded that since China had not changed its policy as a result of one year of U.S. economic threats, "we have reached the end of the usefulness of that policy." But the U.S. Government has imposed an economic embargo on Cuba for more than three decades without changing the policy of Fidel Castro's government. Haven't we reached the end of the usefulness of U.S. policy toward Cuba?

What's more, human-rights abuses in Cuba pale in comparison to those in China. So why the continued embargo on Cuba alongside the clear sailing for China? Because Clinton refuses to stand up to powerful pressure groups, whoever they are. He'll roll over for the anti-Castro lobby just as quickly as he'll roll over for the business-China lobby.

Indeed, he has almost a clinical case of corporate dropsy. Whether the issue is China, NAFTA [North American Free Trade Agreement], GATT [General Agreement on Tariffs and Trade], or even health insurance, Clinton has consistently refused to take on the giant private interests that distort our democracy.

Critics of the Clinton Administration, on the Left as well as the Right, tend to draw sharp—and wholly unwarranted—distinctions between the President's domestic and foreign policies. They praise his focus on domestic concern and disparage his vague dithering on foreign problems. Or they assert that recurrent crises around the world have prevented Clinton from bearing down on his home-front agenda. Such analyses are inept and misleading. The handling of China's human-rights/trade-status equation demonstrates that foreign and domestic considerations are inextricably linked: At home as well as abroad, corporate profits come first and people come last.

9

China's Most-Favored-Nation Status Should Be Revoked

Fang Lizhi

Fang Lizhi is an astrophysicist, author, and one of China's most prominent dissidents. Fang escaped arrest the night of June 4, 1989, when Chinese soldiers massacred hundreds of students and other demonstrators in Beijing's Tiananmen Square. He found sanctuary inside the U.S. Embassy compound and lived there for one year. Fang now lives in exile in the United States and is a physics professor at the University of Arizona in Tucson.

If it continues to maintain China's most-favored-nation trade status (MFN), the United States will be seen by China as a "paper tiger" that will not stand up for the values it represents. This perception will encourage China to develop its military and sell weapons abroad as it sees fit. The best way to get China's leaders to heed the United States is to cancel MFN. At stake is East Asia's stability and the credibility of the United States.

The Chinese leaders have slammed the door closed from the inside. Unless the United States responds now with the cancellation of Most Favored Nation (MFN) trade status [MFN was renewed in 1994 and 1995 without human rights conditions], Beijing will see the United States as the "paper tiger" that [late Chinese leader] Mao Tse-tung always said it was. The failure to react to China's intransigence on human rights will show to the East what the failure to act in Bosnia has meant elsewhere: When push comes to shove the West does not have the will to stand up for the values that it stands for.

That perception will be dangerous for the long run. Feeling free to flout human rights, develop its military might and sell weapons to the world in any way they see fit, an economically powerful China will then pose a threat to the stability of all East Asia.

By detaining and harassing dissidents on the eve of the March 1994

Fang Lizhi, "Call Beijing's Bluff on Human Rights," *New Perspectives Quarterly*, Spring 1994. Reprinted with permission.

visit by U.S. Secretary of State Warren Christopher, whose very purpose was to discuss human rights, China's rulers were trying to show their strength and demonstrate they will not be bullied by the West. They were trying to show that they will not blithely surrender to a new hierarchy of the world order with the United States on top.

When the Chinese leaders ignored a 1993 U.S. plea not to test a nuclear device, thus upsetting a worldwide moratorium on testing, they were putting the United States itself to a test of wills. Their affront to Secretary Christopher was another test of that sort which they think they can get away with because of President Clinton's political troubles over the Whitewater scandal that has consumed Washington. China's rulers are banking on Clinton's perceived political weakness combined with America's strong commercial interests in trade with China to win their bluff.

A brutal ideology

Already the argument is common in business circles that China is "different" than the West because of its Confucian culture and thus should not be subject to the same human rights conditions as the rest of the world.

Well, Taiwan is a Confucian society and its human rights record is far better than Beijing's. The truth is that China's leaders, starting with Deng Xiao Ping, are more Leninist than Confucian. Their power is based not on learned authority or respect for elders, but on the brutal ideology of one party rule. No matter how open the market has become, China's communist rulers have not departed from this principle one iota. They fully understand that to allow the kind of freedom implied by the American pressure on human rights is a direct threat to their hold on power.

The other common argument against cancelling MFN for human rights reasons is that greater trade with the United States will bring a more generalized prosperity to China and that, in turn, will be the basis for more widespread democratic practices.

Here we need only to remind ourselves that in addition to the Leninist element, China's rulers are also invoking nationalism to protect themselves. And, as Japan and Germany bloodily illustrated in this century, nationalism plus economic might without human rights is not the road to democracy; it is the road to fascism.

Nationalism plus economic might without human rights is not the road to democracy; it is the road to fascism.

Finally, [late] U.S. President Richard Nixon often said that good relations must be maintained with China because the West can be better heard talking quietly inside Zhongnanghai (the compound near the Forbidden City where China's leaders live and work) than shouting from beyond the Great Wall.

That may have worked at some point in the past, and it may be true at some point in the future. For now, though, China's leaders aren't listening either way.

The best way to get them to listen now is to cancel MFN while maintaining diplomatic relations so there are open channels of communication. We must remember that MFN did not precede diplomatic relations. It was the other way around. First, Nixon met with Mao in the early 1970s, then, later on, MFN status was bestowed. In the end, China will recognize its own interests and return to the table.

To maintain MFN with China under the present circumstances is tantamount to letting up the pressure. If that pressure is gone, China's leaders will do anything. Harassment of dissidents will then be the least of their crimes.

From my perspective, the present confrontation between the United States and China is akin to the Cuban Missile Crisis during the cold war. If the United States had not forced Cuba and the Soviet Union to back down, global stability would have been threatened.

If the world wants stability in East Asia over the longer term as that region becomes an economic powerhouse, China's bluff must be called today.

As much as President Clinton may want to satisfy America's businessmen and create U.S. jobs in a time of fledgling economic recovery, it would be short-sighted to sell East Asia down the tubes in the bargain. What is at stake today is the future stability of East Asia and the credibility of the West in defending the values that are the essence of its leadership role on the world stage.

10

U.S. Policy Should Stress Chinese Human Rights Protection

Mike Jendrzejczyk

Mike Jendrzejczyk is the Washington, D.C., director of Human Rights Watch/Asia, an international human rights monitoring organization.

America's appeasement of China's hard-liners has reduced any threat of withdrawing most-favored-nation trade status (MFN) to a hollow gesture. Weakening the link between MFN and improved human rights does a disservice to China's citizens, who should be allowed free expression and free association. America must make clear to China's government that it will not tolerate continued human rights violations.

The Chinese government seems convinced that President Clinton will ultimately settle for minimal, superficial human rights concessions in exchange for MFN [most-favored-nation trade status, which the United States considers annually and which was renewed in 1994 and 1995 without human rights conditions]. The crackdown on dissidents is being extended and intensified in part, we [Human Rights Watch/Asia] believe, because Beijing feels it has nothing to lose. The largest trade delegation to ever visit the United States arrived here in April 1994, buying millions of dollars worth of products and offering hundreds of investment projects, determined to "fight trade with trade." Secretary of State Warren Christopher stated, at the conclusion of his disastrous trip to Beijing in March 1994, that there had been a "narrowing of differences." This upbeat assessment was based on the most token gestures and promises offered by the Chinese government—as I will discuss later. Statements such as this create the impression that the Administration's definition of "overall significant progress" on human rights is so elastic as to be virtually meaningless.

A second example of conflicting signals given by the Administration: the initial U.S. reaction to the re-arrest on April 5, 1994, of Wei Jing-

Mike Jendrzejczyk, Congressional testimony before the U.S. Senate Committee on Foreign Relations, Subcommittee on East Asian and Pacific Affairs, *U.S. Policy Toward China*, 103 Cong. 2nd sess., 4 May 1994, 723.

sheng—China's most prominent dissident—was to express "concern" and "regret." As the roundup of dissidents continued, and Xu Wenli was also re-detained on April 8, the White House issued a stronger statement on the following day.[1] But when asked the crucial question of whether MFN could be renewed if Wei Jingsheng remains in detention, the State Department refused to answer.[2] This kind of waffling only strengthens the hand of China's hard-liners, and reduces the threat of MFN withdrawal to a hollow gesture.

At this stage, we cannot imagine how the Secretary of State could make a credible report to the President saying that China had fully met the conditions in the Executive Order [of May 1993 that extended China's trade privileges with the United States for one year].

In fact, in the weeks since the release of our February 1994 report entitled *Detained in China and Tibet: A Directory of Political and Religious Prisoners*, the human rights situation in China has deteriorated further. Religious believers have been rounded up and sent to prison, and peaceful advocates of independence for Tibet have been imprisoned or have had their sentences increased. Poets, film directors, and publishers have been harassed or banned from working. Most troubling has been the frontal assault launched against the renewed dissident movement in Beijing, Shanghai, and other cities. Dozens of activists have been either briefly detained or arrested and are now awaiting prosecution for "ideological crimes."[3]

The expanded crackdown on political and religious dissidents is documented in a report we are issuing today [May 4, 1994], *China: No Progress on Human Rights*, which updates our February survey. Our testimony is based, in part, on this new report.

U.S. policy: maintain the MFN leverage

Human Rights Watch/Asia welcomed the President's Executive Order when it was issued in May 1993, but expressed concern about the vague and loose wording of the human rights conditions contained in the order. We have been dismayed by the conflicting signals given by members of the Administration, which was divided over China policy and was being heavily lobbied to step back from its commitment to link trade and human rights in China.

We are concerned about any perception of a weakening of the President's commitment to condition MFN on human rights improvements. This would seriously undermine U.S. credibility in Beijing—with the American people, who strongly favor conditioning or restricting trade on human rights grounds,[4] and with other foreign governments. U.S. influence on human rights worldwide would be seriously damaged.

Secondly, any weakening of the MFN/human rights linkage would send a devastating message to China's struggling pro-democracy movement. The re-emerging movement has been forming small, informal networks around the country, and is trying to sink roots into the community, calling not only for increased democracy and human rights, but also articulating the pressing concerns of the general public. As the government's economic reforms continue to spark a wide range of severe social and economic dislocations, and the problem of official corruption escalates, pro-democracy activists are calling for increased protection of worker rights and for effective legal remedies against predatory officials. Clearly, political dissent can no longer be dismissed as simply the isolated or marginal concern of a dissatisfied elite.

It is in the interest of stability and peaceful change in China that Chinese citizens now be allowed to exercise their internationally recognized rights of free expression and free association, rather than wait for tensions to build, and risk the possibility of another Tiananmen Square–type massacre in response to a resurgent pro-democracy movement.

Thirdly, it would be dangerous and naive to base U.S. policy on the assumption that economic reform in China will inevitably lead to political change, including an enhanced respect for human rights. China's leaders seem to be doing everything in their power to prevent economic liberalization from leading to political reform. But at the same time, they urgently need MFN and the trade and investment relationship with the United States in order to carry out their aggressive economic reform program. That is precisely why the MFN leverage is so important. We have monitored human rights conditions in Guangdong, Shanghai, and other areas most heavily affected by foreign investment and economic reforms.[5] We have detected no greater respect for civil, political, or religious freedoms in these areas than in any other parts of China.

Over the long term, economic development may help stimulate demands for political reform, but how the government responds to these demands will be conditioned, in part, on how foreign opinion reacts. Given the Communist Party's determination to maintain its rule, and the uncertainties of the post–Deng Xiaoping [China's ailing leader] era, there is no guarantee that trade in itself will automatically improve human rights. Thus, continued international pressure is vital.

It is in the interest of stability and peaceful change in China that Chinese citizens now be allowed to exercise their internationally recognized rights of free expression.

MFN is a blunt tool, but as of yet no one has come up with a viable alternative for effectively pressing the Chinese government to improve its human rights record.[6] We are prepared to look at alternatives to MFN, but *only* alternatives that will continue to exert real pressure on Beijing. To de-link MFN and human rights before that alternative is found is to throw away the most powerful lever we now have for change.

The Administration's conflicting signals on MFN have undercut any credible threat of revocation. This has only increased Beijing's confidence that it will receive MFN regardless of whether it takes actions to improve human rights. Further, China's leaders have been led to believe that by helping the President "save face" by making some token, superficial human rights reforms, they can obtain a commitment from the Administration to effectively de-link MFN from human rights (reverting back to a pre-1989, *pro-forma* annual renewal process as required by Jackson-Vanik [1970s legislation]).

To restore his credibility, the President should immediately appoint a high-level interagency committee to prepare a range of targeted sanctions that could be utilized if China's compliance with the terms of the Executive Order falls short. These options should be examined and made public now—not to undermine the MFN threat, but to give it teeth by showing the President's determination to impose partial sanctions if China makes only partial progress in improving human rights. Secretary Christopher will then feel free to make an honest assessment of progress, leaving it up to the President to decide among a range of policy options that are already in place and fully explained to the Chinese, the Congress, and the American people. We understand that the Administration is, in fact, privately exploring such options.

The Administration should develop a proposal for creatively using carrots and sticks to press for human rights improvements.

We are also concerned that any partial sanctions imposed be significant and more than a token wrist-slapping. To be effective, any such sanctions must be designed to send a clear, unambiguous message to Beijing that it will pay a real economic price for continued human rights violations.

We proposed, in an op-ed article published in the *New York Times*, an across-the-board tariff hike of 10 percent, with further increases possible if China keeps dragging its feet on human rights.[7] The loss of normal trade treatment need not lead to prohibitively high rates (of 30 or 60 percent or higher) that would radically curtail trade. By setting less than a punitive rate, the Administration could ensure that Beijing would feel the pinch, but trade would continue. Transparency and predictability would be relatively easy to maintain. The implementation and monitoring of such a partial sanction would not entail some of the administrative, legal, or technical difficulties posed by some other options. From our point of view, this is definitely the preferred approach.

Other partial sanctions the Administration should consider, all of which have some inherent benefits and drawbacks:

- Raising tariffs on some or all goods produced, manufactured, or exported by state-run enterprises, while maintaining nondiscriminatory treatment on products from "nonstate-owned organizations."[8] This was the approach taken in the Mitchell-Pelosi legislation enacted by both houses of Congress in 1993, but vetoed by then-President George Bush;

- Using the worker rights provision, adopted in 1988, of Section 301 of the Trade Act of 1974, to selectively raise tariffs on certain goods, commodities, or categories of goods, and link this decision to both the lack of progress on meeting the terms of the Executive Order and the flagrant denial of internationally-recognized worker rights in China, especially in light of the recent crackdown on independent labor activists.[9]

We urge the Administration to develop a multilateral policy towards China to augment U.S. bilateral actions on human rights. This would both enhance the effectiveness of U.S. actions, and counter the argument from the Administration's critics that the United States is unfairly shouldering the burden of pressing Beijing to uphold international human rights standards. A long-term policy for dealing with China on human rights during the post-Deng transition is urgently required.

The Administration should develop a proposal for creatively using carrots and sticks to press for human rights improvements. Several European governments—most recently Sweden, plus Australia—have sent human rights delegations to China. These ad hoc initiatives could be strengthened, for example, if the G-7 [Group of Seven] countries [the seven largest industrialized nations] were to collectively urge China to invite the U.N. Working Group on Arbitrary Detentions to undertake investigations and make recommendations, then maintain pressure for their implementation. Contrary to Administration statements, virtually no significant progress was made on the seven items in the Executive Order.

China's political prisoners

On the question of access to Chinese prisons by international humanitarian and human rights organizations, there were ongoing negotiations between the Chinese government and the International Committee of the Red Cross (ICRC), and this was encouraging. However, the ICRC's negotiators left Beijing after the last round of talks in April 1994 without an agreement. [China suspended negotiations that spring.] According to news reports, the ICRC was pressing for access to all detainees, while the Chinese authorities insisted that the discussions focus only on those prisoners convicted of a crime, thus excluding the thousands sentenced administratively, or those detained and held for months or years without trial.

The most important concession thus far was the release on April 23, 1994, of the leading dissident, Wang Juntao, to travel abroad "on bail for medical treatment."[10] The total number of known releases of political or religious prisoners, including Wang Juntao, comes to twenty-five since the Executive Order was issued. Of these, several were freed simply because they had served their full terms. Others, like Wei Jingsheng, have been re-arrested.

Meanwhile, the number of new arrests of peaceful political or religious activists since the Executive Order was issued is well over one hundred. These include:

- A number of activists detained between January and April 1994 for circulating appeals calling for the right to strike and the legalization of independent workers' and peasants' labor unions;

- On April 12, 1994, yet another senior dissident intellectual, Xiao Biguang, age thirty-two, a professor of Chinese literature at Beijing University and a leading figure in the underground Protestant church, was seized by six security officers after his home was searched and books and manuscripts were confiscated. He has not been informed of the reasons for his arrest, nor has his family been allowed to see him. The detention order merely said he had been involved in "illegal activities." Because he was closely associated with labor activist Yuan Hongbing, his arrest may be linked to the crackdown on people involved in the circulation of petitions on labor rights;

- Li Guiren, a fifty-year-old editor and publisher who was released in 1993 on medical parole, was re-arrested on February 16, 1994, despite his extremely serious cardiac problems;

- Tibetan monks and nuns were arrested in connection with two demonstrations in Lhasa on March 21 and on March 27, 1994; several arrested earlier had their sentences extended by as much as eight or nine years;

- Father Wei Jingyi, a priest released from prison in 1993, was again picked up on January 20, 1994, in Xushui County, Hebei Province;

- Zhou Guoqiang was "detained for investigation" by security officials on March 3, 1994, due to his activities "organizing illegal gatherings in October 1993." (This refers to his role in drafting a "Peace Charter" calling for democratic reforms that was made public at the time of President Clinton's meeting with Chinese President Jiang Zemin in Seattle in November 1993.)

Trials of dissidents are also continuing. Secret trials in February or March 1994 resulted in draconian sentences given to a reporter for a Hong Kong newspaper, Xi Yang, sentenced to twelve years in prison; and a clerk at the People's Bank, Tian Ye, sentenced to fifteen years in prison. Both were accused of spying and stealing state financial secrets. The verdict in Xi's case sparked demonstrations in Hong Kong and official protests by the Hong Kong Journalists' Association.

On April 20, 1994, in Beijing, another journalist went on trial: Gao Yu, who had been arrested in October 1994, one day before she planned to come to the United States to begin a fellowship at the Columbia University School of Journalism. She was charged with "providing information to organizations outside the border," and was allegedly charged with obtaining a copy of a top secret speech by [Chinese president] Jiang Zemin. (Her case was on the list presented to the Chinese government by Assistant Secretary of State for Human Rights John Shattuck in October 1993; the Chinese response, in the information given to Mr. Shattuck in February 1994 as part of the so-called "accounting," was merely to place her name in a category of persons "not convicted of a crime.")

Most of the political prisoners with serous medical problems on the list of about twenty such cases presented by Mr. Shattuck in October 1993 remain in prison.[11] They include, for example, Bao Tong, sixty years old, who has been detained under harsh conditions for over four years; he was transferred to a Beijing hospital, but his family now fears he may be suffering from cancer.

During Assistant Secretary Shattuck's trip to Beijing in late February 1994, he was given some information on prisoners in partial response to lists he had submitted in October 1993. Those lists contained the names of 341 people detained or restricted due to their political or religious beliefs. The Chinese response is so thin on detail and so inaccurate it is virtually useless as an "accounting" of prisoners, as required by the Executive Order. It provides minimal information until now unavailable on only *five people:* (1) Abduweli, listed among sentenced prisoners; he was known to have been arrested but not known to have been sentenced; (2) Gao Yunqiao, sentenced to death with a two-year reprieve; the Chinese now list him as sentenced, apparently meaning the sentence was commuted; (3) Bayantogtokh, believed to have been imprisoned in Inner Mongolia; the Chinese now say he was released; (4) Wang Manglai, also imprisoned in Inner Mongolia; the Chinese say he was released under the name Wa Manglai; (5) Abdurrezzak, according to the Chinese, was released on medical parole/suspended sentence; this was previously unknown.

Of the 341 names, the Chinese have promised information on 106 Tibetans, and responded only 235. But the Chinese claimed they were unable to identify approximately a third of these. (This includes, for example, well-known dissidents now in prison or detention, such as Zhang Yafei and Chen Yanbin, student leaders sentenced in March 1991.) In those cases where the Chinese acknowledged individuals were detained or released, no information was provided on their whereabouts, charges, or lengths of sentences. The names are simply divided into eight categories that are so broadly labeled they are utterly devoid of meaning. (Our new report contains a more detailed assessment of the Chinese government's response.)

The Administration should refuse to accept this faulty, so-called "accounting," and we would repeat our earlier recommendation that the State Department should also seek a meaningful accounting for all of the 3,317 cases the Chinese government officially acknowledges have been convicted of "counterrevolutionary" crimes.[12]

Forced labor

A mandatory condition in the Executive Order deals with cooperation on implementing the U.S.-China agreement on prison labor exports.

During his visit to Beijing in January 1994, Secretary of Treasury Lloyd Bentsen announced that the U.S. Customs Service was being given permission to visit five suspected prison labor sites under the terms of the MOU (Memorandum of Understanding) signed by the United States and China on August 7, 1992. Secretary Bentsen also said that measures to ensure more effective implementation of the MOU had been agreed to in principle, but no agreement was signed.[13]

Among the five sites to be visited were facilities such as the Shanghai Laodong Machinery Factory and the Shanghai Laodong Steel Pipe Works. Requests to visit these prison factories had been made as early as 1992 but were denied, and we suspect that by the time any inspections have taken place, the Customs Service will find little that is worth inspecting.

During Secretary Christopher's trip, a new agreement on prison labor was signed ("Statement of Cooperation on the Implementation of the MOU"), an implicit recognition by the United States that the Chinese have been stonewalling and have not been living up to the terms of the first agreement. Will the promises of better cooperation in this agreement be worth anything more than those made in the previous agreement? Until the Customs Agency and State Department provide a full report on how the Chinese have responded to at least fifteen outstanding requests for information and/or inspections, this is impossible to assess. We believe that nothing short of frequent, unannounced visits will help ensure that prison labor goods are no longer being exported to the United States. And I would note that the agreement on textile exports reached with

China on January 18, 1994, does allow U.S. officials to conduct surprise inspections of Chinese companies suspected of engaging in illegal trans-shipments. Why was the Administration not just as tough in demanding stricter compliance with the prison labor MOU?

Human Rights Watch/Asia continues to document the use of forced labor in China, and the use of political prisoners to make products for export purposes.

Congress should insist on tangible, measurable progress and a dramatic improvement in the level of cooperation by Chinese authorities. In the meantime, I would simply note that the agreement *is* a step forward in that it stipulates that requests for information or inspections by the United States should be met within sixty days. The original MOU had no such time frame.

However, the agreement is not without loopholes. For example, in paragraph 5, on page 2, the Chinese side is required to furnish "relevant" records and materials, and to arrange inspections of "necessary areas" of the prison facility or labor camp. But who will determine what is "relevant" and "necessary"? In the case of some previous inspection requests, the United States was simply told that certain facilities or portions of facilities were "not open to the public," and therefore inspections were not "necessary."

Human Rights Watch/Asia continues to document the use of forced labor in China, and the use of political prisoners to make products for export purposes. A forthcoming report will include some of the latest information we have available on inhumane prison conditions and forced labor for export, including a first-person account by a former prisoner.

[*China: No Progress on Human Rights*] documents the case of thirty-one members of a Protestant church sect in Shandong Province who were arrested in a fierce crackdown in May–June 1992; the sect's meeting was broken up, participants arrested, and their church building bulldozed. The leaders were arrested and given stiff sentences. We now know that the local leader, Zheng Yunsu, sentenced to twelve years in prison, is being held at the Shengjian Motorcycle Factory (actually, a prison enterprise). Most of the twenty-five other sect members are performing forced labor at Shandong Province No. 1 Labor Education Center, working in a clay mine that exports its products to the United States, Japan, and other markets.[14]

A former political prisoner from that same labor camp, now in the United States, has provided to us and to the Customs Service a graphic account of the conditions there, including exhausting work, numerous accidents, rudimentary medical care, and the beating of prisoners who fail to meet production quotas or are considered insubordinate.

Notes

1. Dee Dee Myers said the Administration was "deeply troubled" by the crackdown and urged the Chinese government "to release immediately (those persons) detained or imprisoned for the peaceful expression of their views." (Reuters).

2. See Mike McCurry, State Department regular briefing, April 7, 1994. Q. "Could the Clinton Administration renew MFN with him (Wei) in detention?" A. "I don't want to address that question."

3. See, for example, "China: New Arrests Linked to Worker Rights," *Asia Watch*, vol. 6, no. 2, March 11, 1994.

4. A *Wall Street Journal* poll cited a majority of 65% and Potomac Associates, by 60%.

5. See *Detained in China and Tibet* for examples. Shanghai has been the scene of particularly harsh repression recently.

6. For example, some have proposed a bilateral commission on human rights, as a forum to discuss human rights cases and to press for general improvement in human rights in China. We do not believe such a commission could serve any useful purpose, except as a public relations exercise that could be used to deflect public criticism. A bilateral commission would simply interpose another layer between the two governments, already engaging in a direct, bilateral human rights dialogue, and would provide the Chinese government with further opportunities for stonewalling and bureaucratic inertia.

7. "Squeeze China—By Degrees," by Holly Burkhalter, *New York Times*, March 29, 1994.

8. According to the World Bank, exports of nonstate sector enterprises, including urban and rural collectives, private enterprises, individual businesses and foreign-invested firms, plus township and village enterprises, accounted for a minimum of 40 percent of China's total exports or 50 percent of its manufacturing exports in 1992, with the bulk of nonstate enterprise exports coming from the coastal provinces. *China: Foreign Trade Reform*, pgs. 14–15, The World Bank, April 1, 1994.

9. The 1988 amendment includes in the definition of "unreasonable" trade practices any policies or acts which constitute a persistent pattern of conduct that "denies workers the right of association . . . the right to organize and bargain collectively (and) permits any form of forced or compulsory labor." [Section 1301, (d)(3)(B)].

10. Human Rights Watch/Asia warmly welcomed this long-overdue humanitarian step, but we are concerned that the 13-year prison term Wang received in 1991 has not been lifted. Thus he could be reimprisoned any time should he return to China and be deemed to have committed "further offenses."

11. Released on medical parole: Zhao Pinju (mid-June 1993), Ding Junze (Feb. 1994), Wang Juntao (April 1994).

12. Our report, *Detained in China and Tibet*, contains the names of 1,200 so-called "counterrevolutionaries."

13. Human Rights Watch/Asia is not opposed to prison labor *per se*, but we do oppose forced labor which is forbidden by international standards; we object to political prisoners being assigned to perform forced labor, also a violation of international norms, and condemn human rights abuses such as beatings, atrocious prison conditions, and inhumane treatment—all common features in China's prison factories and labor camps.

14. See *China: No Progress on Human Rights*, Appendix, page 26, for a listing of their names and whereabouts.

11
U.S. Policy Tolerates China's Wrongdoings

William P. Hoar

William P. Hoar is the Washington editor of the New American, *a bi-weekly magazine that promotes conservative ideals.*

America ignores a host of abuses by Communist China. A U.S. State Department human rights report charged that there continued to be widespread and well-documented human rights abuses in China in 1994, including arbitrary and lengthy detention, torture, forced labor, and other mistreatment of prisoners. The report also mentioned China's forced abortions and sterilizations under its one-child-per-family population policy. China also regularly steals patented and copyrighted material from the West, producing illegal versions of automobiles, computer software, and videos. In committing these abuses, China has little to fear from America, which seeks to accommodate rather than confront Beijing.

Headlines in early February 1995 notwithstanding, there was a lot less to the U.S. trade war with Beijing than one might expect. The threatened imposition of the largest trade sanctions in U.S. history against Communist China hardly stopped the Clinton Administration's business with that oppressive regime.

Even with the Clinton Administration's threatened imposition of 100 percent tariffs on more than a billion dollars worth of Chinese products, as well as similar retaliation by Beijing, negotiations between the two countries were back on track within days: Energy Secretary Hazel O'Leary went ahead with plans to bring big business leaders to mainland China to consummate some $8 billion in deals for power plants and other technology; there was approval of a rocket deal; and the U.S. government pressed ahead with yet another arrangement to assist the Chinese in purchasing a million tons of grain at subsidized prices.

On January 1, 1995, even as Beijing was imposing hefty taxes and duties on "luxury" goods imported by foreign enterprises, the United States removed tariffs on many Chinese goods imported to the United States.

William P. Hoar, "Firing Blanks in the Trade War," *New American*, March 20, 1995. Reprinted with permission.

That move will save Beijing an estimated $2 billion, or twice as much as the threatened sanctions.

In May 1994, breaking another campaign promise, President Clinton again gave Red China access to U.S. markets as a "most favored nation" (MFN), and even delinked its notorious human rights abuses from MFN status. One State Department official, speaking of China's dismal human rights record, admitted, "We believe that, frankly, it has deteriorated since the MFN renewal last May." Winston Lord, Assistant Secretary of State for East Asia and Pacific Affairs (and former president of the Council on Foreign Relations), has similarly admitted that the human rights situation has suffered, with the regime "rounding up dissidents, harassing them more."

Increased abuse

Just before the dramatic announcement about the "trade war," which was precipitated over intellectual property rights, not human rights, the State Department's annual human rights report to Congress was published, putting the lie to President Clinton's claim of May 1994 that abandoning the economic weapon of MFN "gives us the best chance of success on all fronts." According to the State Department report, the Red Chinese have stepped up abuse of rights on all fronts.

"In 1994," reported the State Department document,

> there continued to be widespread and well-documented human rights abuses in China, in violation of internationally accepted norms, stemming both from the authorities' intolerance of dissent and the inadequacy of legal safeguards for freedom of speech, association and religion. Abuses include arbitrary and lengthy incommunicado detention, torture and mistreatment of prisoners.

It is, acknowledged State (which in these matters gives the benefit of the doubt to the communists), "impossible to determine the number of extrajudicial killings by [Red Chinese] government officials in 1994." The Chinese representative to the UN Human Rights Commission, seeing what passes for trumps in U.S. public discourse, responded that such charges are nothing more than "new racism."

The State Department noted that there was a lack of proper accounting of those missing or detained after the 1989 Tiananmen Square massacre. Among other abuses State noted were: a crackdown on newsmen; arrests of dissidents; denials of fair trials; and mandatory work in the labor camps, called *laogai*. Henry Wu, a veteran of the *laogai* (where beatings and starvation are part of the regular punishment meted out for not meeting work quotas), estimates that there are 7.5 million in these brutal camps, six times the 1.25 million admitted by Beijing. The State Department also took notice of reports of prisoners being forced to donate body organs for transplants.

There is also mention in the report (though hardly enough) of China's forced abortions and sterilizations. Representative Chris Smith (R-NJ), chairman of the House International Relations subcommittee on human rights, has taken State to task for downplaying the latter, saying that, as in past years, the report "seems to excuse the excesses of the brutal [People's Republic of China] policy by pointing with alarm to the size of China's population."

Ominously, Beijing, whose official policy is one child per family, launched a new, strict "family planning" program—as widespread killing of preborn babies (and born, for that matter) has apparently not been enough. The new policy, as explained by the New China News Agency, includes stipulations that if a rural couple has but one child, the government will provide "special treatment in supplying fine seeds, information, technical training, and funds so as to raise their incomes to a level higher than the local average."

Because of cultural and governmental discrimination against girls, there are 114 recorded male births in Red China for every 100 recorded female births. Selective sex abortion is partially to blame for this, as is "high early female mortality" (as it is called euphemistically in a Stanford research study). Western population "experts" generally avert their eyes from the "controversial" methods by which Beijing seeks to limit Red China's population.

Profligate pirating

As noted earlier, piracy is behind the latest trade dispute. For example, Red China, which regularly steals patented and copyrighted material from the West, filches up to 98 percent of the software for its computers, including most found in government buildings—all while mouthing platitudes against the theft and with a law (passed in 1993 during an earlier "crisis" with the United States) specially directed against such practices.

Disregard for property rights is widespread. Chrysler was about to make a $1 billion minivan deal with Beijing when it noticed that the Chinese were already copying its Jeeps. In another automotive area, China held out a billion-dollar contract as a counter to threatened sanctions, saying that if there were no trade war, Ford or GM would be chosen as a partner with Shanghai Automotive Industry Corporation. Otherwise, negotiations would likely resume with the Japanese.

> *Red China, which regularly steals patented and copyrighted material from the West, filches up to 98 percent of the software for its computers.*

Communist China may have the third largest market in the world—and upwards of $50 billion in trade with the United States—but the Reds are dependent on others, especially the United States (which is China's largest customer), though Washington acts as if Beijing holds the upper hand. While U.S. exports to China (where the average annual wage is $419 in the city, $216 in villages, and $106 in rural areas), grew from $3 billion in 1979 to $9 billion in 1994, the mainland has expanded exports to the United States from $3.1 billion in 1979 to $38 billion in 1994. Not counted is the estimated $3 billion that the United States loses to pirated goods.

Although the Clinton Administration professed to be surprised and relieved when the Chinese acquiescence came hard on the February 26,

1995, deadline, the threatened tariffs would have affected only about 1 percent of Red China's imports. Sanctions were set up to be narrow and minimally detrimental to either side. Left out from potential U.S. tariff punishment were such items as electronic components and toys, while the Chinese side didn't hit, for example, airplanes from the United States. Beijing threatened to keep out U.S. movies. But, since it only permits in ten titles per year (legally, that is), that is largely meaningless. Similarly, extra tariffs on U.S. cigarettes wouldn't amount to much because so many are already smuggled into China.

Sidewalk vendors of pirated goods tell reporters that they are provided with pirated merchandise by the communist state itself.

What was slated for increased tariffs in the U.S. gesture? Such relatively trivial items as "footwear with outer soles of rubber, plastic, leather or composition leather (other than house slippers, work footwear or tennis shoes, basketball shoes and the like, for misses) valued at over $2.50 a pair." That'll make the Long March veterans [Chinese] quake!

The markets in China, made to appear so desirable in the West, still come under the thumb of the communist government. Sometimes that thumb is heavy. For instance, an estimated 40 percent of the resources of the central government prop up large and inefficient state-run companies, reports *Business Week*, which continue to dominate about half of the economy. In order to stave off unemployment, state-run banks continue to loan funds to these dinosaurs. Meanwhile, those producing pirated CDs, software, and videos are often the children of party members, provincial party members, or others with political ties to Beijing. Sidewalk vendors of pirated goods tell reporters that they are provided with pirated merchandise by the communist state itself. Of course, when it is necessary, the state cracks down on some hapless vendors or factories.

Bellicosity unchecked

The contention that one can buy a friendly policy from communists is particularly inappropriate with Red China. Beijing's military, in fact, has directly taken over a business empire of its own, estimated to garner up to $20 billion annually. All the better to project power in, say, the Spratlys—an island group in the South China Sea, thought to have large oil resources, to which various claims have been made by Red China, Taiwan, and Vietnam, as well as Malaysia, Brunei, and the Philippines. Manila recently complained that Red China had taken over part of its claimed area.

China's growing military strength has helped it to exert pressure on neighboring countries. The communist nation recently took delivery on the first of four new submarines acquired in a billion-dollar deal with Russia, according to *Jane's Defence Weekly*. It has also been selling military equipment to such terrorist-supporting nations as Iran.

When it suits, the Reds simply thumb their noses at us: Beijing still refuses to admit it has given missile parts to Pakistan. Moscow, a beneficiary of U.S. aid, in turn is in the process of selling rocket motors to Red China that can be used in its cruise missiles. When the United States objected, as the *Washington Times* reported, Russia pointed out that a Phoenix-based firm in 1994 sold similar technology to Beijing that the CIA believes could be used in long-range cruise missiles. In addition, Senator Jesse Helms (R-NC) has pointed out the inconsistency of Administration objections to sales of atomic reactors to Iran by Russia and China, noting that Washington set the example with a North Korean nuclear deal.

Still with an eye to assimilating Taiwan, by force if necessary, Beijing in 1994 gave more hints of its intentions by holding military exercises, including landings, on islands near Taiwan. Indicating their displeasure at a slight improvement in relations between Washington and Taipei [Taiwan's capital], the Red Chinese cancelled a visit from U.S. Transportation Secretary Federico Peña because he had earlier stopped in Taiwan.

Meanwhile, attention has been focused on the power plays likely to ensue with the death of Red China's ailing 90-year-old leader, Deng Xiaoping, and whether his hand-picked successor Jiang Zemin will actually wind up in the driver's seat. Many think that, in order to shore up his internal position, Jiang will have to be even tougher on Washington.

Whoever winds up in the driver's seat, the Reds have little to fear from the Clinton Administration, which already puts up with China's theft and lying. Despite the occasional headline about worsening relations, American accommodation seems the byword. Red China, for instance, wants to be in the World Trade Organization. While that may not happen right away, Beijing has patience. The long-range goal, says the State Department's Winston Lord, is "to integrate China into the world community."

12

America Should Prepare for China's Military Threat

Thomas L. McNaugher

Thomas L. McNaugher is a senior political scientist at the RAND Corporation think tank in Washington, D.C. He is the author of several books and papers on America's military.

America should be concerned with China's growing power. Leaders in China are becoming assertive, making claims on bordering territories and building a modernized military. This assertiveness, China's uncertain intentions, and the growth in wealth China promises to create in East Asia pose a security dilemma for neighbors in Japan, Taiwan, Vietnam, and elsewhere. A stronger China could threaten U.S. interests in a stable and peaceful East Asia, and America itself could be drawn into regional disputes. Furthermore, questions of arms sales and violations of weapons treaties by China and the United States make both sides uneasy. Relations between the two nations will hinge on power, and America should strive to retain a good deal of strength.

East Asians don't know quite what to make of China these days. Their expanding involvement in China's rapidly growing economy is making them rich. But it is also helping to make China strong. Leaders in Beijing are already claiming border areas and offshore islands with a new assertiveness and buying weapons from Russia capable of backing those claims with force. As one Singaporean diplomat told American researcher David Hitchcock in 1993, "All of Southeast Asia is scared" by the growth of China's power.

Americans too seem to be worrying more about China. Beside long-standing concern about China's arms sales to "backlash" states and its poor human rights record now stand visions of China as an "awakening dragon" preparing to assert its dominance in East Asia. Samuel Huntington writes of a Sino-centric Confucian civilization headed for conflict with the West—a threatening China that must be contained, much as the Soviet Union was during the Cold War.

Thomas L. McNaugher, "A Strong China: Is the United States Ready?" *Brookings Review*, Fall 1994. Copyright 1994, The Brookings Institution. Reprinted by permission.

How seriously should we take the notion of a "threat" from China? Alarmists would seem to be exaggerating. China's military is huge but also vastly underdeveloped doctrinally and technologically. That will change if present trends continue, but recent double-digit economic growth, while striking, is probably unsustainable. At least as plausible as an "awakening dragon" is a China plagued by economic decentralization and political decay and thus unable to exploit its enormous power potential. Finally, since 1978 China's leaders have sought a stable and friendly international environment to encourage economic growth. They have solved their once-rancorous border dispute with Russia and shelved their territorial disputes with India. Far from being a threat, today's China would seem to confirm liberal claims that economic growth and interdependence encourage cooperation and conflict resolution.

Yet China's growth is indeed worth worrying about, not because it will surely continue, nor because a strong China will seek to dominate its neighbors, but because *if* China continues to grow it will confront the world with a change in power relationships of unprecedented size, ultimately involving the emergence of a power capable of overshadowing Japan, perhaps even the United States. In the past, large power transitions have been marked by instability and conflict. China's ties to the global economy may soften this one. But if not, China's growth is likely to threaten regional stability—a vital U.S. interest—regardless of China's intent.

China's growth is already tweaking insecurities around East Asia. And while East Asians will try to cooperate in balancing and containing China's power, lingering suspicions and an underdeveloped regional security structure obstruct such alliances. Although China is years away from posing a serious direct military threat to the United States (assuming it wants to), the destabilizing effects of its growth could easily find their way to the U.S. doorstep.

Are U.S. policymakers ready to deal with an increasingly strong China? They have no historical precedents on which to draw for guidance, since for much of U.S. history China was in decay or collapse, while during the Cold War China remained in the shadow of Soviet power. Today U.S. policymakers have the same problem China's neighbors do. They are happy to help China get rich, since the process adds to U.S. wealth. They just wish that making China rich did not also make it strong. Alas, China may grow strong anyway. It is doing so now, and its emerging strength is already straining U.S. policy responses. It's time to think through the implications of a strong China.

The dilemma of China's growth

Even though China's leaders profess to threaten no one, China's military growth ensnares its neighbors in a classic "security dilemma." Unsure of China's intentions, changeable in any case, they look at China's capabilities. And these, now huge but backward, are growing more worrisome.

Availing itself of Russia's willingness to sell weapons at bargain-basement prices, China is modernizing its forces *and* extending their range. Alongside newer tanks are long-range fighters, a more seaworthy navy, and more sophisticated amphibious assault capabilities. Such purchases reflect mid-1980s doctrinal changes emphasizing greater mobility and firepower for ground forces and projection capabilities for sea and air forces. Against the background of Mao's doctrine of people's war, which relied largely on infantry defense, the new trend in weapons and doctrine inevitably appears threatening.

Ironically, Russians are among those most worried. Russia's vastly underpopulated Far East has always been a logistics nightmare for Russian forces. Against a strong China, Russians worry that their Far Eastern border is almost indefensible. That problem helps explain the conspicuous absence of a nuclear "no-first-use" pledge from Russia's new military doctrine. Like NATO [North Atlantic Treaty Organization] during the Cold War, Russians think they may have to rely on nuclear weapons to compensate for conventional force inferiority.

Above all, China has time—if it continues to grow. In that case it will slowly outstrip its neighbors in economic as well as military might.

China's fledgling arms buildup has also begun to stir Japanese anxiety about vital sea-lanes in the South China Sea. Reportedly Japanese diplomats have warned Moscow about its arms sales to China. They may also have threatened economic retaliation had China purchased an aircraft carrier from the Ukraine (China has dropped the carrier idea, at least for now, although its reasons remain unclear). The U.S.-Japan security relationship allays concern in Tokyo, but any withering of that relationship while China's force buildup continues could start a Sino-Japanese arms race.

For some of China's neighbors, the security dilemma posed by China's growth is compounded by ancient territorial disputes. Japan, China, and Taiwan, for example, all claim a small island group (called Diaoyutai in China, Senkaku in Japan) northeast of Taiwan. A potentially much more serious dispute involves Outer Mongolia, independent now but part of China two centuries ago. At times in this century Chinese leaders as diverse as Sun Yat-Sen, Mao Tse-Tung, and Chang Kai-Shek all referred to Outer Mongolia as part of "greater China," and in 1921 China tried to back its claim by force, but was repelled by Soviet troops. Today Beijing recognizes the Republic of Mongolia, but Outer Mongolians, shorn not only of occupying Soviet forces but of a strong Russia to play off against a growing China, still worry.

For the moment, the "front-burner" dispute involves the Spratly islands, on the southern edge of the South China Sea. Its historical claim sharpened by its interest in the offshore area's minerals, China claims all these islands and thus virtually all the South China Sea. But Taiwan, Vietnam, Brunei, Malaysia, and the Philippines claim at least some of the same islands and undersea resources.

Beijing has promised not to use force to settle the dispute and has declared itself willing to co-develop the area's resources with other claimants, but its actions undermine its rhetoric. For twenty years China has slowly extended its occupation of various islands southward. It used force in 1974 and again in 1988 to wrest key islands from Vietnam. And it has continued developing military bases in the area. In February 1992 China's People's

Congress claimed the Spratlys more forcefully than ever before, authorizing military action to defend those claims. China also hired a U.S. firm to explore for oil on islands on what Vietnam claims is its continental shelf.

It is correct but not very comforting to other claimants to note that China's military remains underdeveloped, even in comparison with many Southeast Asian militaries. China doesn't need aircraft carriers to assert authority in the South China Sea; it has proximity and island bases. It doesn't need sophisticated tanks to worry the Russians; it has relative mass. China's 1979 invasion of northern Vietnam may have been a tactical debacle, but it was strategically successful, when combined with China's support to Cambodia's Khmer Rouge, in squeezing Vietnam between threats in two directions.

Above all, China has time—*if* it continues to grow. In that case it will slowly outstrip its neighbors in economic as well as military might. The uncertainty helps explain the low-key reaction of China's neighbors to the Spratlys dispute. They are buying arms, at least partly because of concern about China, but too slowly yet to call the purchases an "arms race." Most have also deployed forces and built military bases or even resort hotels on their islands to buttress their claims. Vietnam has asked U.S. firms to explore for oil around the islands it occupies. Still, with China growing, its intentions uncertain, and its growth a source of wealth to all, no one in Southeast Asia is anxious to stir the pot too much.

The time factor may also explain China's resistance to Indonesian efforts to internationalize the Spratlys discussion. Its neighbors understandably see Beijing's insistence that the dispute must be settled by claimants alone as an attempt to prevent them from seeking help while China's position in bilateral negotiations grows ever more formidable.

China and its neighbors

Some Southeast Asians are, in fact, seeking help from the United States. Vietnam's contracts with U.S. oil firms suggest a subtle effort to involve the U.S. government in its Spratlys dispute. President Fidel V. Ramos of the Philippines has been more direct, arguing that the U.S.-Philippines mutual security treaty commits U.S. forces to defend his country's island claims. Others are ambivalent about U.S. help. Yet all are likely to take the U.S. response to more assertive Chinese actions as a litmus test of U.S. resolve and commitment to their security.

Thus far the United States has demurred, rejecting Ramos's treaty interpretation and warning U.S. firms that they explore disputed areas at their own risk. U.S. diplomats repeat endlessly that "no one should use force" to resolve these issues. With North Korea's nuclear program, Japan's security debate, and a host of trade issues crowding their East Asian agenda, U.S. policymakers understandably want to stay clear of a local dispute over tiny, desolate, and often submerged atolls.

Yet clearly the Spratlys dispute could threaten U.S. interests in a stable, open, and peaceful East Asia. The worst case, as recently described by Mark Valencia of the East-West Center, would be more frequent and violent clashes that could endanger shipping and eventually involve the United States or Japan. More likely but only slightly less worrisome would be continued stalemate, increasing tension, and the gradual emergence of an arms race around the South China Sea.

More broadly, growing Chinese assertiveness and military strength could strengthen hawks in Japan's ongoing security debate, in turn raising tensions among Japan's neighbors. And a souring of Sino-Russian relations could encourage Moscow to refurbish its nuclear doctrine, imperiling the arms control agreements fashioned as the Cold War ended. A growing China can threaten U.S. interests even if it means to threaten no one, and long before it can threaten the United States directly.

The United States is already involved in handling the effects of China's growth through its security ties to Japan and South Korea. It may become more deeply embroiled sooner than it thinks, for East Asians are unlikely to be able to handle these problems by themselves. For most East Asians, China is simply too big to handle alone; even the Russians feel vulnerable. Although China's neighbors might band together to balance China's power, especially now, with China still relatively underdeveloped, regional security cooperation is also underdeveloped. Deep underlying suspicions hamper cooperation in Northeast Asia, where close U.S. allies like Japan and South Korea prefer dealing with the United States to dealing with each other.

The Southeast Asians have ASEAN (the Association of Southeast Asian Nations, embracing Indonesia, Singapore, Thailand, Malaysia, the Philippines, and Brunei), which, since its founding in 1967, has gradually expanded both the range of issues it can discuss and the outsiders it includes. But the expansion process has been painfully slow and could easily fail to keep up with serious regional security problems. Besides, ASEAN scarcely controls the major power relationships around it. Its members work to keep the United States engaged in the region partly to sustain a stable balance within which they can operate with some freedom.

The United States and a strong China

The possibility that the United States will be pulled into regional disputes involving China suggests a compelling need to collect the fragments of U.S.-China policy—the concern for trade one day, arms transfers the next, help with North Korea the next—into a more coherent whole. The difficulty of predicting China's future is no excuse for ignoring the implications of China's continued growth.

The challenge is especially great since the United States, despite its own strength, has been consistently uncomfortable with the prospect of a strong China. This was true even during the Cold War, when China helped the United States counter Soviet power. A communist power, indirectly a recent enemy in Vietnam, and a direct threat to Taiwan, China was not the most cooperative of strategic partners. Beijing resented U.S. support to Taiwan, feared U.S. inconsistency, and was reluctant to curtail its own freedom of action by tying itself closely to the United States. After 1982 each country tended to go its own way, China to a more balanced stance between the superpowers, the United States to a more Japan-oriented anti-Soviet policy.

As the need for strategic cooperation declined, tensions in the relationship began to rise. Some had to do with China's internal behavior, notably its human rights abuses. But others—concern about the growing

U.S. trade deficit with China, for example, or about China's arms sales to unsavory Middle Eastern regimes—were grounded in skepticism about the kind of international citizen China intended to be.

Even the human rights debate, so prominent after the Tiananmen crackdown in 1989, was not without strategic content. Those wishing to curtail China's most-favored-nation (MFN) trade status with the United States were saying, in effect, either that the United States should not help China grow strong or that it should help only if China's behavior met certain standards. Some continued to define those standards in terms of China's international behavior—its arms transfers and trade surplus. But even those most concerned with human rights expected a more democratic China to be better behaved internationally.

The human rights–trade link [applied to MFN renewal by Bill Clinton in 1993, but removed in 1994] was based partly on the assumption that, with the Cold War over, China was weak and strategically unimportant; with strategic allies, after all, Washington handles human rights issues quietly and behind the scenes. Whether that assumption was true at the time (the Soviet Union's collapse actually increased China's regional power by removing a threat), it isn't now, as President Clinton's 1994 move to sever the link suggests. If the United States wants to deal with a growing China, it will have to refine its tools for doing so.

China and arms control

Indeed, it will have to drop more than the "sledgehammer" of curtailing China's trade status. Long before they raised this threat, U.S. policymakers sought to induce China's adherence to various global arms control agreements by offering or refusing to license the export of U.S. high technology, in effect offering to help China grow strong so long as it agreed to play by established rules of "good" state behavior. The effort never worked that well and is probably outrunning its usefulness.

To be sure, China has slowly become more involved in arms control. In 1980 it sent its first delegation to the disarmament conference in Geneva, where its negotiators have become increasingly involved in shaping agreements like the Chemical Weapons Convention and the Comprehensive Test Ban Treaty. Nor has China been completely unwilling to sign certain agreements—especially those that constrain others besides itself. Thus it signed the Outer Space Treaty in 1984 to slow a superpower "space race" that might have degraded its nuclear forces. But it has refused to negotiate nuclear arms control, since to do so might ultimately hobble its top-priority but still relatively underdeveloped nuclear weapons program.

Problems arise for the United States in the range of agreements that lie between the easy and the unacceptable. The Non-Proliferation Treaty (NPT) and the Missile Technology Control Regime (MTCR) would cut China's lucrative sales of nuclear and missile technology and marginally curtail its ability to support old allies (Pakistan) and new friends (Iran, Syria). Here U.S. technological inducements have affected China's commitment to arms control. But they have had less effect on China's behavior.

China finally joined the International Atomic Energy Agency in 1984 to gain access to U.S. commercial nuclear power technology then being denied by a Congress deeply suspicious of China's attitude toward proliferation. Although China did not then join the NPT, its leaders stated publicly that they would not engage in nuclear proliferation, and privately that they would not help Pakistan's nuclear weapons program. According to U.S. intelligence reports, however, they continued to do precisely that. When Beijing finally joined the NPT in 1992, again in return for U.S. high-tech sales and also in response to world outrage about the post–Desert Storm exposure of Iraq's massive clandestine nuclear weapons program, reports of illicit sales to Pakistan continued.

Perhaps tensions between the United States and China on arms control are only to be expected.

A similar pattern of halting entry and spotty compliance has marked China's acceptance of the MTCR, to which Beijing committed itself late in 1991 as part of the same high-tech deal that brought it into the NPT. China reportedly canceled prospective missile sales to Syria and Iran. But evidence of continuing Chinese missile technology exports to Pakistan forced President Clinton to invoke U.S. sanctions in August 1993.

Some would not hold Beijing responsible for illicit arms sales, arguing that the sales are often conducted by relatives of China's ruling elite, who operate beyond the control of the Foreign Ministry. Yet precisely because they are related to China's rulers, these operators could presumably be brought to heel if those rulers cared enough to do so.

At the other extreme are critics who see Beijing as a rogue state that, in the words of Senate staffer William Triplett, "has violated every nonproliferation pledge it has ever made." Yet this charge, while partially true, overlooks the distance Beijing has come—from revolutionary power opposed to arms control to a "semi-status-quo" power that has signed several arms control agreements and complies with some, if not all, of them. Unless we write cases of compliance off as deception (which some do—this is, after all, a civilization for which deception is a key strategic virtue), there is more of a puzzle here than China's critics admit.

Established power, growing power

Perhaps tensions between the United States and China on arms control are only to be expected. The established rules of international conduct, written by the strong and naturally favoring their interests, are likely to be resented by *any* rising power. Thus the NPT freezes nuclear inequality in place, and any nuclear arms control talks would also likely assure China's current inferiority. And the MTCR forbids missile sales (among China's few marketable military technologies) while leaving U.S. aerospace firms free to market sophisticated aircraft worldwide.

Small and weak states, destined always to be rule takers rather than rule makers, may have to accept this situation and satisfy their interests as best they can. By contrast, rising powers, especially one with China's proud past, recent growth rates, and enormous potential, have every reason to resist agreements that reflect current power relationships in hopes of negotiating from a stronger position down the road. This seems to be

Beijing's approach to the Spratlys.

But the United States is too powerful and potentially dangerous to be put off. Besides, its technological inducements have been useful. And if some of the rules the United States proffers appear unfair to the Chinese, others may be growing more attractive as economic growth increases China's stake in the prevailing status quo. China's spotty record of compliance with arms control may reflect the ambiguities of this situation.

But cheating has also been a form of power—a risky one, but perhaps the only one available to China at its current stage of development. Take China's illicit links to Pakistan. Rather than vehemently denying accusations that it continues to sell missile components to Pakistan, Beijing has instead offered to discuss those sales if the United States will discuss its 1992 decision to sell F-16s to Taiwan. Evidently the Clinton administration has agreed to this linkage. Cheating has opened the chance for leverage over a weapons deal China staunchly opposes.

It is time Americans . . . prepare[d] for the possibility of a China stronger than any they have seen before.

For now, U.S. officials will do no more than listen politely but then ignore China's arguments, as they have in the past. But past practice may have a limited future, since the stakes in this game are changing in China's favor. Growth and global involvement are reducing China's need for U.S. technology, while the collapse of the Soviet Union has reduced the urgency of China's search for technical advance. For the United States, on the other hand, the end of the Cold War has made proliferation more worrisome than ever. It will be increasingly difficult to "buy" China's agreement with dribs and drabs of U.S. technology. As is the case with the F-16 sale, China will want U.S. strategic concessions in return for concessions of its own.

Which raises the larger issue at stake here. China's argument that missiles and sophisticated strike aircraft are equally dangerous and ought to be jointly controlled—a position that may well be analytically valid—was excluded from the MTCR talks in the interest of simplicity and practicality. In forging a link between its missile sales and the U.S. F-16 sale to Taiwan, Beijing is forcing its broader argument back onto the agenda. To the extent that it succeeds, it will be leaving the realm of rule takers and entering the world of rule makers.

The United States has been willing to see China help write rules that play to U.S. interests, like the Chemical Weapons Convention. But is it ready for such help on subjects dear to its heart? Is it ready to curb its own arms sales, now far and away the world's largest and a key source of income for the shrinking U.S. defense industrial base, in return for curbs on China's? Is it ready to limit the size, type, or operational freedom of its own forces in East Asia in return for limits on China's force modernization? These questions are far-fetched now, but perhaps not for long.

Obviously ambitious strategic agreements are worse than useless if Beijing cannot be trusted to keep its word. But that argument goes both ways. China's leaders regard the U.S. F-16 sale to Taiwan as a violation of the 1982 U.S.-China Communiqué on Taiwan, by which Beijing *thought* it had gained limits on such sales. In fact, the United States has consistently reinterpreted the Communiqué to suit the needs of Taiwan's defense, hungry U.S. defense firms, or presidents campaigning for reelection. A recent Senate move to elevate the Taiwan Relations Act above the Communiqué, virtually nullifying the latter, was softened only by last-minute executive branch lobbying. Surely if the United States can tailor its understanding of signed agreements to its loyalty to an old ally, Beijing can tailor its reading of the MTCR to its continued support to Pakistan?

Despite expressions of outrage over the F-16 sale, China's leaders were not surprised by the move. Strong states, they know, do what they will, while weak states do what they must. Behind moralizing U.S. rhetoric they see a state that does what it will, fashioning agreements to suit its interests and reinterpreting them when convenient. China's leaders take a realpolitik view of the world. No doubt they will "do what they will" if and as their country grows more powerful. Meanwhile, they have every incentive to justify their own arbitrariness by referring to U.S. behavior.

Again, the immediate issue is Taiwan; China's continued growth will make it increasingly difficult for the United States to sustain the studied ambiguities of its policies toward Taiwan and the People's Republic. And the general point applies across the range of activities where U.S. and Chinese interests potentially collide. If U.S. officials want to ground U.S. relations with China in rules—whether tacit or codified in elaborate agreements—they are going to have to abide more honestly by rules themselves. Beijing will happily be a mirror, reflecting U.S. misbehavior in its actions, with penalties that grow as China grows.

China may misbehave anyway; treating it more equitably only maximizes the prospects that it will not. Thus until we know a great deal more about China than we do today, the complement to a more equitable U.S. approach to the country will be continued U.S. strategic engagement in East Asia and vigilance over China's actions. Whether China chooses to become the expansionist dragon some expect or instead seeks the cooperative relationship with the United States that China's leaders say they want, the currency of the relationship will be power, and that means the United States had best keep a good deal of it on hand. If China's leaders conclude that the U.S. military is leaving East Asia in any case, why should they take the United States any more seriously than the United States now takes them?

Ironically, if the challenge to Americans today is merely to think of China as a potential equal, should China actually exploit its raw potential, Americans will find themselves challenged merely to maintain equality! That day may never come (perhaps the sheer enormity of the prospect helps explain why many Americans hope it does not). But economic growth and changed strategic circumstances have already made China's increasing power a potential threat to U.S. interests. It is time Americans began to adjust their policies, and more importantly their perspectives, to prepare for the possibility of a China stronger than any they have seen before.

13

The United States Should Crack Down on Chinese Espionage

Malcolm McConnell

Malcolm McConnell is a roving editor for Reader's Digest *monthly magazine.*

Espionage by Chinese nationals in the United States increasingly threatens America's security. Spy operations, numbering more than one hundred, have successfully pilfered advanced military hardware and top-secret information. These Chinese-funded spies are gaining access to sensitive computer, military, and nuclear technology by holding legitimate jobs in American universities and laboratories and by creating dummy corporations. America does not take this threat seriously enough, often deporting Chinese spies rather than seeking criminal prosecution.

When Wu Bin, a slender, bespectacled 28-year-old philosophy instructor in Nanjing, received a visa to work in America in 1990, he went to Norfolk, Va., a major naval and defense contracting center. Instead of remaining at the company designated on his visa, however, he dropped out of sight.

In 1992 Wu resurfaced, opening the office of Pacific Basin Import-Export Co. in nearby Virginia Beach with Li Jing Ping, the owner of Comtex International, ostensibly a small electronics firm in the same town. Li was a former official of China's Ministry of Finance. He was aided by Zhang Pinzhe, a former diplomat who was supposedly here as an English student at nearby Old Dominion University.

Pacific Basin and Comtex looked into the purchase of sensitive military-electronics components that were illegal to export without a license under the Arms Export Control Act. Within weeks, Wu was contacted by a front company operated by China's Ministry of State Security (MSS), which controls that nation's espionage activities.

In March 1992, Comtex began purchasing image-intensifier tubes from Varo, Inc., near Dallas. The tubes were the heart of night-vision sights used on America's newest tanks and helicopter gunships. Their export is strictly prohibited without a government license.

After disguising the tubes as medical equipment, Li and Wu shipped them to a Chinese front company in Hong Kong. From there the tubes went to mainland China. Soon, with Zhang's help, Pacific Basin also began exporting the technology to the same front company.

Suspicious about Pacific Basin, U.S. Customs obtained search warrants, staked out the company's office, subpoenaed its phone records and reviewed its bank records. The connection between Pacific Basin and Comtex was uncovered, and in October 1992 the spies were arrested.

In June 1993, Wu Bin, Li Jing Ping and Zhang Pinzhe were convicted of violating the Export Control Act. Wu and Li were also convicted of money-laundering, Zhang of conspiring to money-launder. Wu received a ten-year sentence and his accomplices shorter terms. The case is under appeal.

Extensive spy operations

Wu's well-funded spy operation was only part of a large-scale Chinese effort to steal American military secrets. Nicholas Eftimiades, an analyst with the Defense Intelligence Agency and author of *Chinese Intelligence Operations*, writes that because China does not pose a credible military threat outside Asia, its espionage activities go largely unchecked. He reports that the MSS has dispatched or recruited hundreds of Chinese nationals as spies, making it the most active foreign power engaged in the illegal acquisition of American technology. Moreover, Chinese students and scholars who return home are routinely debriefed by Chinese intelligence.

Not all espionage authorities agree with Eftimiades's view of the threat. But Raymond Wannall, former assistant director of the FBI for counterintelligence, calls Chinese espionage "a tremendous and growing threat to America." He adds, "Today, China has the largest foreign presence in America in which to conceal its spies."

John F. Cooper, a professor of international studies at Memphis's Rhodes College, says many Chinese operatives take jobs in university institutes and corporate research laboratories, where they patiently work their way up until they gain access to sensitive information.

[China is] the most active foreign power engaged in the illegal acquisition of American technology.

Other spies, like Wu Bin, pose as legitimate businessmen, buying high-tech hardware through dummy companies. Wannall estimates that well over 100 such fronts have been opened in the past decade, overwhelming U.S. law enforcement and customs surveillance resources.

These agents are following the trail blazed by Soviet high-tech spies in the 1970s. Among Moscow's successes were the theft of plans for infrared guidance systems for antimissile defense, and guidance systems for cruise missiles. The Soviets also used stolen American technology to upgrade their weapons plants. Paul Godwin, professor of Chinese defense and security policy at the National War College, is among those who believe Beijing also is hoping to build a military-industrial complex that can one day produce ultra-sophisticated weapons.

The goal, says James Lilley, former American ambassador to Beijing and assistant secretary of defense for international security, is to project power into Asia, then eventually onto the global stage. For its neighbors, "China is emerging as the greatest security concern in the region," agrees Desmond Ball, one of Australia's foremost defense experts.

The threat to our allies and to America's own security interests in Asia is real. For decades, the U.S. Seventh Fleet had nothing to fear from the Chinese navy's coastal patrol boats and diesel-powered submarines. These obsolete vessels avoided contact with our Navy. But today, following a modernization drive unprecedented in China's history, fast new Chinese-built turbine-powered destroyers, frigates and nuclear subs—being deployed with sophisticated "vertical-rising" torpedoes capable of sinking Western carriers—range far from the Chinese coast, and their subs have shadowed Seventh Fleet formations. China has also built air and naval installations on islands in the South China Sea in order to press its territorial claims there and, according to intelligence sources, has been given access to island bases in the Indian Ocean by Myanmar (formerly Burma).

While the Chinese navy does pose a threat to its neighbors, Rear Admiral Eric McVadon (Ret.), former defense and naval attaché in Beijing, says, "the U.S. Navy could easily defeat it in battle because of our superior size and technology. The real concern," says Admiral McVadon, "is that the United States might be drawn into a regional conflict."

The nuclear threat

Another ominous threat is nuclear. Defense and intelligence experts confirm that the newest versions of China's powerful Dong Feng ("East Wind") intercontinental ballistic missile are targeted on American cities and military bases. The authoritative *Jane's Strategic Weapon Systems* confirms that the missile has a range of some 9000 miles, capable of striking cities in the continental U.S.

Many authorities maintain that these developments should be viewed within the Asian context. Notes Seth Cropsey, former deputy Undersecretary of the Navy in the Reagan and Bush Administrations, "It is more likely that Washington and Beijing will square off over the issue of whether there is to be a dominant power on the Asia landmass."

But others sound an alarm. "The Chinese are engaged in an unprecedented espionage campaign and nuclear-weapons buildup," warns Sen. Larry Pressler (R., S.D.), a member of the Senate Foreign Relations Committee. "But I can't get senior Clinton Administration officials to acknowledge the threat."

Adds San Francisco Congresswoman Nancy Pelosi (D., Calif.), a member of the House Intelligence Committee, "China is engaged in a full-court press to obtain American high technology to modernize its military." She notes that California's Silicon Valley is a "regular stop" for official members of Chinese delegations, in spite of restrictions that limit access to the area. Yet, Pelosi warns, both the Bush and Clinton Administrations "have turned a blind eye to this practice."

The full range of Chinese espionage has been uncovered only in the past decade. In September 1988, China exploded a "neutron" bomb whose intense radiation can kill even the crews of heavily armored tanks. Western observers had considered the weapon beyond the reach of Chinese technology. They were right. The FBI confirmed that the Chinese government had obtained crucial data about the weapon from the Lawrence Livermore National Laboratory, a nuclear-weapons facility outside San Francisco. An investigation by the General Accounting Office revealed that the Department of Energy had permitted more than 100 Chinese scientists to visit US. weapons laboratories in the previous two years.

Experts confirm that the newest versions of China's powerful . . . intercontinental ballistic missile are targeted on American cities and military bases.

Says Douglas Paal of the Asia Pacific Policy Center, Chinese spies continue to target American institutions where defense research is conducted. "Our university research labs are wide open."

The theft of nuclear-weapons secrets and sophisticated computer technology is only part of the Beijing offensive. Wannall says China mounts hundreds of smaller operations aimed at stealing the latest conventional weaponry, frequently using "sleeper agents" like Kao Yen Men, who burrow into U.S. society and are not activated for years.

Kao, now 56, first visited the United States in 1971. As a Hong Kong citizen, his movements within America's Chinese communities drew little notice. Opening a restaurant in Charlotte, N.C., he traveled frequently to the People's Republic of China and to Hong Kong, where he said he had a small export business.

In 1987, Kao met with Ron Blais, a private investigator in Charlotte who had retired after 20 years in the Army. Kao, whose English was still poor, needed a trustworthy American to help steal a Mark 48 ADCAP torpedo, the Navy's deadliest submarine weapon.

Kao promised Blais over $100,000 if he obtained the torpedo. After feigning interest, Blais went to the FBI. Over the next six years, he secretly recorded Kao on audio- and videotape discussing a long procurement list of advanced American military hardware, including the Mark 48 and the jet engines used in the F/A-18 Hornet, the Navy's newest fighter.

Blais even met Kao in Beijing. There, Kao's superiors told Blais they would pay $4 million in cash for the F/A-18 engines alone.

Last December, the FBI arrested Kao. But he was arraigned in immigration court rather than in a criminal proceeding; critics maintain the Clinton Administration was concerned that a criminal trial could harm U. S.-China relations. So instead of prison, he was simply deported—a treatment often meted out to Chinese spies.

Lenient treatment is often justified on the ground that a public trial will reveal counterintelligence methods. But deporting agents rather than jailing them gives the Chinese an invitation, notes one counterintelligence authority: "Come and spy. The worst that will happen is that you'll be kicked out of the country."

William Triplett II, former Republican counsel to the Senate Foreign Relations Committee and a top expert on China, calls such leniency outrageous. "China is the only country in the world still pointing nuclear weapons at America," he notes. "Yet when we catch their spies, we slap them on the wrist."

Most counterintelligence experts agree. The first step in thwarting Chinese espionage is recognizing the threat. But President Clinton, like President Bush before him, sees China primarily as a trading partner undergoing desirable economic and political reform. This makes exposing the full scope of Chinese spying politically difficult. The Administration wants closer ties with China, counterintelligence experts say. But the closer the ties, the more opportunities for espionage.

"We're crazy to accept this," Triplett says. "Our government must get tougher with Chinese espionage and prosecute every spy to the full rigor of the law."

14

China Is Unlikely to Protect American Intellectual Property Rights

Frankie Fook-lun Leung

Frankie Fook-lun Leung is an attorney with the law firm of Lewis, D'Amato, Brisbois, and Bisgaard in Los Angeles and a lecturer of law at Stanford Law School in California.

Counterfeiting of American and other copyrighted products such as compact discs proliferates in China, where pirated goods successfully compete with authentic products. Knockoff products come from factories owned, operated, or protected by government enterprises, making protection of intellectual property rights virtually impossible. The resistance of China's provinces to central government orders against counterfeiting adds to the problem. A February 1995 U.S.-China agreement on intellectual property rights protection will not make much difference. Protection will occur only if copyright piracy harms China's own economy.

During my nine years of law practice in Hong Kong, where I did a modicum of enforcement litigation on intellectual property rights, I marveled at the ingenuity with which counterfeiters violated the law.

First, unlike a reputable U.S. producer of compact discs—who would abandon a mold after processing a certain number of CDs, in order to maintain quality control—a pirate would use the same mold until it was no longer usable. The pirate's best work would produce 100 CDs that would be sold at $10, with those of secondary caliber fetching $9 and third-rate ones selling for $8; those of the lowest quality might still be sold for $1. One commonly finds the $1 products at swap meets, the $9 products at top-notch department stores and the others in between. The counterfeiters use a seemingly more effective economy of value of pirated products.

Second, pirated brand-name products sold by peddlers would definitely not attract customers who truly wanted to buy authentic products.

Frankie Fook-lun Leung, "Tradition of Copying in China Fuels the Piracy of Intellectual Property," *Los Angeles Times*, March 5, 1995. Reprinted with permission.

83

However, it is a grave error to ignore the pirate's unlawful activities in the belief that a brand-name product sold at the high-end market would never be undermined.

Piracy multiplies exponentially like a malignant growth. A pirate's ability to upgrade the quality of his fake products is absolutely mind-boggling. An infringer's products can quickly compete with the authentic products on equal terms and eat into the top end of the market.

China certainly shares the characteristics of many developing countries in its record of violations of intellectual property laws. In the 1960s and '70s, Taiwan was a leading pirate of U.S. vinyl records and college textbooks. Purchasing the Taiwanese edition of Samuelson's *Introduction to Economics* was the common practice adopted by most students taking introductory economics in Hong Kong and Taiwan in the 1960s. The books sold at about a tenth of the price of the authentic U.S. edition. Similarly, today it is beyond the purchasing power of most Chinese consumers to pay $20 for a U.S.-manufactured CD.

A surge of consumerism

Any visitor to China or Southeast Asia witnesses the relentless drive of the people to possess consumer items: a color television, a radio, an air conditioner. That same pride of ownership is an attitude Western capitalism actively promotes, though it is taken for granted in the West.

As elsewhere, people in the East want to acquire CDs and listen to them at home. Driven by this unprecedented emergence of pride of ownership, increasing material affluence, a surge of consumerism and the West's efforts to transplant its culture—including music and lifestyle—markets for fake products such as pirated CDs are proliferating.

This is no reason to condone blatant violations of intellectual property laws. Nonetheless, it explains the economic force driving the spread of illegal trading.

American copyright owners are particularly exasperated in China, because unlike Taiwan or Thailand—where counterfeiting is committed in the private sectors—the production of pirated products in China has actually come from factories owned, operated or protected by state-owned or quasi-state-owned civilian and military enterprises.

The role of the government in manufacturing renders the eradication of violations virtually impossible.

The role of the government in manufacturing renders the eradication of violations virtually impossible. Nor can the courts be relied on to enforce any crackdown on piracy. In the city of Zuhai in southern China, sheriffs who reportedly attempted to enforce court decrees or judicial orders of confiscation were sabotaged by local government officials.

Another cultural facet of piracy in China is that, traditionally, copying has been neither condemned nor illegal. On the contrary, many apprentices of Chinese art copy a master's works or emulate them as closely as they can. Doing so is considered an acceptable and time-honored learning process. Such a cultural mindset provides an additional incentive for training copycats and diminishes any sense of guilt.

The pressure exerted on China by U.S. Trade Representative Mickey Kantor to stop piracy is further mitigated by the uncontrollable decentralization of authority in China.

Many of the edicts issued by the central government are practically ignored—if not circumvented—by the provincial governments, particularly in the affluent coastal southern provinces such as Fujian and Guangdong, where most of the counterfeiting takes place.

Indeed, efforts by the United States to compel China to enforce its own intellectual property laws are destined to run into the same problems already besetting the Chinese government, which is genuinely inadequate to do the policing on its own. For all its pledges of tough enforcement, the agreement reached between the two countries in February 1995 will hardly make a difference.

Rather, tangible changes will come about only if China's widespread piracy harms the country's own economy. That has already taken place in Taiwan, where piracy of domestic products raises enough concern for the local industrialists to put pressure on their government to enforce the law.

Until that happens in China—after another decade or longer—all the fine agreements put on paper by the two countries will not solve the piracy problem.

Organizations to Contact

The editors have compiled the following list of organizations concerned with the issues debated in this book. The descriptions are derived from materials provided by the organizations. All have publications or information available for interested readers. The list was compiled on the date of publication of the present volume; names, addresses, and phone numbers may change. Be aware that many organizations take several weeks or longer to respond to inquiries, so allow as much time as possible.

Asian Studies Center
Claremont Institute
250 W. First St., Suite 330
Claremont, CA 91711
(909) 621-6825
fax: (909) 626-8724

The center, part of the conservative Claremont Institute think tank, studies cultural, economic, and political issues that affect China and other Asian countries. It supports strong ties between the United States and China. The center publishes books, reports, and studies, including the papers "Made in the Chinese Laogai: China's Use of Prisoners to Produce Goods for Export" and "The People's Republic of China and the Security of East Asia."

Asia Pacific Policy Center (APPC)
1730 Rhode Island Ave. NW, Suite 1011
Washington, DC 20036
(202) 223-7258
fax: (202) 223-7280

APPC is a nonprofit institution that seeks closer defense, political, and trade ties between business and political leaders in the United States and East Asia. The center does not engage in lobbying or advocate a particular agenda; instead it offers pragmatic, issue-by-issue analysis of U.S.-Asia trends. Its activities include informal consultation and briefing between government policymakers and corporate or other institutional executives. APPC publishes the weekly *Issue Brief* and occasional report-length publications.

The Asia Society
725 Park Ave.
New York, NY 10021
(212) 288-6400
fax: (212) 517-8315

The society offers workshops and sponsors study missions, conferences, and seminars about Asia for the public. Its publications include the quarterly *Asia Newsletter*, the annual *China Briefing*, media background papers on Asia, and books and videos.

Center for Chinese Studies
University of California
Berkeley, CA 94720-2318
(510) 643-6321
fax: (510) 643-7062

The center is a research institute that studies Chinese culture and politics. In addition to offering lectures on China, the center publishes a variety of research papers, including the China Research Monograph series.

East Asian Institute
420 W. 118th St.
New York, NY 10027
(212) 854-2592
fax: (212) 749-1497

Sponsored by Columbia University, the institute is a forum for research scholars, including faculty members, research associates, visiting scholars, professional fellows, and doctoral candidates. Its publications include the Studies of the East Asian Institute hardcover series, the Occasional Papers of the East Asian Institute paperback series, and shorter *Institute Reports*, including "Recent Developments in China's Relations with Russia and the United States" (April 1995).

Embassy of the People's Republic of China
2300 Connecticut Ave. NW
Washington, DC 20008-1724
(202) 328-2580
fax: (202) 588-0032

The embassy serves as China's representative in the United States. It provides the public with information on China, including press releases and the bimonthly *Newsletter*.

Human Rights Watch/Asia
1522 K St. NW, Suite 910
Washington, DC 20005
(202) 371-6592
fax: (202) 371-0124

This division of Human Rights Watch monitors and reports human rights abuses in Afghanistan, Burma, Cambodia, China, and other Asian nations. It keeps abreast of U.S. compliance with laws requiring human rights considerations in foreign policymaking. It sponsors fact-finding missions, disseminates results, and publishes the bimonthly *Human Rights Watch* newsletter.

National Committee on United States–China Relations (NCUSCR)
71 W. 23rd St., 19th Fl.
New York, NY 10010
(212) 645-9677
fax: (212) 557-8258

The committee is a nonprofit educational organization that encourages understanding of China and the United States among citizens of both nations. It is involved in educational and policy activities in such areas as economic management and development, international relations, legal affairs, and mass communications as they relate to the People's Republic of China, Hong Kong, and Taiwan. Its publications include the pamphlets *The Evolution of Greater China and What It Means for America* and *Sino-American Military Relations: Mutual Responsibilities in the Post–Cold War Era.*

Office of the United States Trade Representative (USTR)
600 17th St. NW
Washington, DC 20506
(202) 395-3230
fax: (202) 395-4809

USTR is responsible for the direction of all U.S. trade negotiations and for the formulation of trade policy. The office publishes the annual reports *Annual Trade Agenda* and *National Trade Estimate Report* and makes documents related to trade available to the public.

State Department Watch
PO Box 65398
Washington, DC 20035
(703) 241-3700

State Department Watch is a nonpartisan foreign-policy watchdog group concerned with U.S. State Department's and other federal agencies' actions regarding American foreign policy. It lobbies Congress and meets with corporate leaders in an attempt to increase human rights in China and to end the export of goods manufactured by Chinese prisoners. Its publications include the monthly *Newsletter* and documents and reports on human rights in China.

United States–China Business Council
1818 N St. NW, Suite 500
Washington, DC 20036
(202) 429-0340
fax: (202) 775-2476

The council is a research and lobbying organization that represents American companies conducting business in China. It provides consulting services to member corporations and holds periodic conferences. The council publishes the bimonthly magazine *China Business Review.*

United States Global Strategy Council (USGSC)
1800 K St. NW, Suite 1102
Washington, DC 20006
(202) 466-6029
fax: (202) 331-0109

USGSC is an organization of individuals interested in international and strategic affairs. It studies the strategic planning and decision-making process of the executive and legislative branches of the U.S. government. The council promotes the strengthening of relations between the United States and China and publishes the bimonthly *China and Pacific Rim Letter.*

Bibliography

Books

A. Doak Barnett et al. — *U.S. China Policy: Building a New Consensus.* Washington, DC: Center for Strategic and International Studies, 1994.

Warren I. Cohen — *America's Response to China: A History of Sino-American Relations.* 3rd ed. New York: Columbia University Press, 1989.

Deng Maomao — *Deng Xiaoping, My Father.* New York: BasicBooks, 1995.

Jurgen Domes et al. — *After Tiananmen Square: Challenges for the Chinese-American Relationship in the 1990s.* Washington, DC: Brassey's, 1990.

Nicholas Eftimiades — *Chinese Intelligence Operations.* Annapolis, MD: Naval Institute Press, 1994.

R. Bates Gill — *Chinese Arms Transfers: Purposes, Patterns, and Prospects in the New World Order.* Westport, CT: Praeger, 1992.

Merle Goldman — *Sowing the Seeds of Democracy in China: Political Reform in the Deng Xiaoping Era.* Cambridge, MA: Harvard University Press, 1994.

Marshall Green, John N. Holdridge, and William N. Stokes — *War and Peace with China.* Bethesda, MD: Dacor Press, 1994.

Harry Harding — *A Fragile Relationship: The United States and China Since 1972.* Washington, DC: Brookings Institution, 1992.

Jie Chen — *Ideology in U.S. Foreign Policy: Case Studies in U.S. China Policy.* Westport, CT: Praeger, 1992.

Samuel S. Kim, ed. — *China and the World: Chinese Foreign Relations in the Post–Cold War Era.* Boulder, CO: Westview Press, 1994.

James R. Lilley and Wendell L. Willkie, eds. — *Beyond MFN: Trade with China and American Interests.* Washington, DC: AEI Press, 1994.

Ramon Hawley Myers — *Thoughts on U.S. Foreign Policy Toward the People's Republic of China.* Stanford, CA: Hoover Institution, 1994.

William H. Overholt — *The Rise of China: How Economic Reform Is Creating a New Superpower.* New York: Norton, 1993.

Robert G. Sutter — *China in World Affairs: U.S. Policy Choices.* Washington, DC: Congressional Research Service, 1995.

Tan Qing-shan — *The Making of U.S. China Policy: From Normalization to the Post–Cold War Era.* Boulder, CO: Lynne Rienner, 1992.

90

William T. Tow   *Building Sino-American Relations: An Analysis for the 1990s.* New York: Paragon House, 1991.

U.S. House of   *The U.S.-China Intellectual Property Rights Agreement:*
Representatives   *Implications for U.S.-Sino Commercial Relations.* Washing-
Committee on   ton, DC: Government Printing Office, 1995.
International Relations

U.S. Senate Committee   *U.S. Policy Toward China: Hearing Before the Subcommittee*
on Foreign Relations   *on East Asian and Pacific Affairs.* Washington, DC: Gov-
                         ernment Printing Office, 1994.

Periodicals

Amy Borrus   "Eyeball to Eyeball with China," *Business Week*, February 20, 1995.

Warren Christopher   "Comprehensive Engagement in U.S.-China Relations," *U.S. Department of State Dispatch*, April 24, 1995.

Congressional Digest   "U.S. Relations with China: 1995–96 Policy Debate Topic," August/September 1995.

Ralph A. Cossa   "Twenty-first Century China: Friend or Foe?" *Strategic Review*, Spring 1994. Available from U.S. Strategic Institute, Kenmore Station, PO Box 618, Boston, MA 02215.

CQ Researcher   "U.S.-China Trade," April 15, 1994. Available from 1414 22nd St. NW, Washington, DC 20037.

William Theodore   "The New Confucianism in Beijing," *American Scholar*,
De Bary   Spring 1995.

Karl W. Eikenberry   "Does China Threaten Asia-Pacific Regional Stability?" *Parameters*, Spring 1995. Available from U.S. Army War College, Carlisle Barracks, Carlisle, PA 17013-5050.

Robert S. Greenberger   "Taiwan, Trying to Win Status in Washington, Targets Grass Roots," *Wall Street Journal*, May 16, 1995.

Harry Harding,   "The Promise and Peril of China After Deng Xiaoping,"
Ronald Montaperto,   *Heritage Lectures*, No. 499, 1994. Available from the
and Anne Thurston   Heritage Foundation, 214 Massachusetts Ave. NE, Washington, DC 20002-4999.

William P. Hoar   "Calming the Red Rage," *New American*, July 10, 1995.

Richard C. Hottelet   "China and U.S.: One Goliath Takes On Another," *Christian Science Monitor*, August 4, 1995. Available from 1 Norway St., Boston, MA 02115.

Skip Kaltenheuser   "China: Doing Business Under an Immoral Government," *Business Ethics*, May/June 1995.

Louis Kraar   "The Risks Are Rising in China," *Fortune*, March 6, 1995.

David L. Lampton   "America's China Policy in the Age of the Finance Minister: Clinton Ends Linkage," *China Quarterly*, September 1994.

Martin L. Lasater

"China and Taiwan: The Need for Balance," *World & I*, April 1995. Available from 3600 New York Ave. NE, Washington, DC 20002.

Susan V. Lawrence

"Beijing's Mixed Message," *U.S. News & World Report*, February 20, 1995.

Brett C. Lippencott

"China Should Adhere to Rules of the Road," *Backgrounder Update*, No. 243, March 29, 1995. Available from the Heritage Foundation, 214 Massachusetts Ave. NE, Washington, DC 20002-4999.

Winston Lord

"Intellectual Property Rights and U.S.-China Relations," *U.S. Department of State Dispatch*, March 27, 1995.

Natasha Ma

"Sino-Sellout," *Toward Freedom*, April/May 1995. Available from 209 College St., Burlington, VT 05401.

Jim Mann

"U.S. Starting to View China as Potential Enemy," *Los Angeles Times*, April 16, 1995. Available from Times Mirror Square, Los Angeles, CA 90012-3816.

Robert A. Manning

"Clinton and China: Beyond Human Rights," *Orbis*, Spring 1994.

Robert A. Manning

"Starting Over: From MFN to a China Policy for the Future," *Policy Report,* no. 20, May 1994. Available from the Progressive Policy Institute, 316 Pennsylvania Ave. SE, Suite 555, Washington, DC 20003.

Steven Mufson

"The Beijing Duck: What U.S. Companies in China Aren't Doing for Human Rights," *Washington Post National Weekly Edition*, April 17–23, 1995. Available from 1150 15th St. NW, Washington, DC 20071.

Seth Mydans

"American Deported from China Kept Secret Diary of Life in Jail," *New York Times*, August 26, 1995.

Aryeh Neier

"Watching Rights," *Nation*, May 22, 1995.

Karsten Prager

"Bulls in the China Shop," *Time*, June 5, 1995.

William Safire

"China's 'Four Fears,'" *New York Times*, May 22, 1995.

Michael Schrage

"China Trade Truth: Copyrights, Human Rights Can't Be Separated," *Los Angeles Times*, February 9, 1995.

Elaine Sciolino

"China's Prisons Forged Zeal of U.S. Crusader," *New York Times*, July 10, 1995.

Robert A. Senser

"Will China Kick the Habit? Lessons from Piracy," *Commonweal*, May 5, 1995.

Nancy Bernkopf Tucker

"Wanted: A Sensible American China Policy," *Christian Science Monitor*, July 18, 1995.

World Press Review

"U.S.-China Compromise," April 1995.

Xiao Qiang

"Needed: Helsinki Accords for China," *Wall Street Journal*, March 3, 1995.

Zhang Kai

"Democratic Struggles Resurge," *International Viewpoint*, July 1995.

Index

Abdurrezzak (political prisoner), 61
abortions, forced, 65-66
Action Plan. *See* State Council
  Intellectual Property Enforcement
  Action Plan
AFL-CIO, 36
America's Interests in China's Environment
  (Murray), 15
Arafat, Yasser, 32
arms control, 74-77
  see also military, growth of Chinese;
  nuclear arms
Arms Export Control Act, 78, 79
The Art of War (Sun Tzu), 43
ASEAN (Association of Southeast Asian
  Nations), 15, 73
Asian Development Bank, 15
Asia-Pacific Economic Cooperation
  summit (APEC), 26, 31
Asia Pacific Policy Center, 81
Asia Watch, 35, 37
Association of Southeast Asian Nations
  (ASEAN), 15, 73
AT&T, 49-50
Atlantic Council, 20

Ball, Desmond, 80
Bao Tong, 60
Bayantogtokh (prisoner), 61
Bentsen, Lloyd, 61
Blais, Ron, 81
Boeing Corp., 49
Bush, George, 34, 50, 58, 82
Business Week, 67

Carter, Jimmy, 34
Castro, Fidel, 51
Central Intelligence Agency, 68
Chemical Weapons Convention, 74, 76
Chen Yanbin, 61
Chi (Chinese official), 40
Chiang Kai-Shek, 71
China
  and arms control, 74-77
  cooperation necessary on intellectual
    property rights, 44-48
  espionage by, in United States, 78-82
  as fastest-growing market in world, 13
  human rights violations in, 35-37
  importance of Security Council
    membership, 11
  military ties with U.S., 41-43

new authoritarianism of, 13
poses military threat to U.S., 69-77
seeks U.S. cooperation on
  economic agenda, 15-16
  educational exchanges, 16
  international agenda, 16-17
  technology agenda, 16
  see also human rights; intellectual
    property rights; military, growth of
    Chinese; most-favored-nation (MFN)
    trade status; nuclear arms
China: No Progress on Human Rights, 56,
  62
Chinese Intelligence Operations
  (Eftimiades), 79
Christopher, Warren, 23, 35, 50, 53, 55,
  58, 61
CIA, 68
Civil and Criminal Procedure Laws
  (China), 44-45
Clinton, Bill, 10-11, 14, 26, 28-31, 39,
  43, 49-51, 54, 60, 74, 82
  on most-favored-nation status, 23-25
cold war, end of
  impact on U.S. foreign policy, 10, 38
communications, and human rights,
  36-37
Comprehensive Test Ban Treaty, 74
Comtex International, 78
Cooper, John F., 79
Council on Foreign Relations, 65
Cropsey, Seth, 80

Defense Intelligence Agency, 79
democratization
  importance to U.S. policy, 11-13
Deng Xiaoping, 12, 28-29, 53, 57, 68
Department of Energy, U.S., 81
Detained in China and Tibet, 56
dual-use technology, 16, 21

East-West Center, 72
Eftimiades, Nicholas, 79
environment, China and the, 15
espionage, by China, 78-82

Fang Lizhi, 52
FBI, 81
Finn, James, 34
Ford Motor Co., 66

Gao Yu, 60

Gao Yunqiao, 60-61
the Gap, 49
General Accounting Office, U.S., 81
General Agreement on Tariffs and Trade
    (GATT), 17, 51
General Motors Corp., 66
Global Environment Facility, 15
Godwin, Paul, 79-80
Greene, Graham, 38
Group of Seven (G-7), 59

Harland, Bryce, 26
Helms, Jesse, 68
Hitchcock, David, 69
Hoar, William P., 64
Hong Kong
    reversion to China, 14, 28
human rights
    and communications, 36-37
    and forced abortions/sterilizations,
        65-66
    importance of to U.S. policy, 11-13
    and MFN status. See most-favored-
        nation (MFN) trade status
    and political prisoners, 20, 35, 56,
        59-61
    and prison labor, 14, 23, 51-62
    property rights are more significant, 65
    trade helps, 36-37
Human Rights Watch/Asia, 55-56, 62
Huntington, Samuel, 69

import substitution strategy, 16
intellectual property rights, 14
    China unlikely to protect, 83-85
    China pays lipservice to, 66-67
    cooperation necessary on, 44-48
    more significant than human rights,
        65
International Committee of the Red
    Cross (ICRC), 27, 59
International Federation of Phonogram
    Industries (IFPI), 46
International Olympic Committee, 17

Jackson-Vanik Act, 57
Jane's Defence Weekly, 67
Jane's Strategic Weapon Systems, 80
J.C. Penney, 49
Jendrzejczyk, Mike, 55
Jiang Zemin, 26, 39, 60, 68

Kantor, Mickey, 44, 85
Kao Yen Men, 81
Kapp, Robert, 30
Kissinger, Henry, 50
K-Mart, 49

Laodong Machinery Factory, 61

Laodong Steel Pipe Works, 61
laogai (prison camps), 65
Lawrence Livermore National
    Laboratory, 81
Leung, Frankie Fook-lun, 83
Li Guiren, 60
Li Jing Ping, 78-79
Lilley, James, 80
Lord, Winston, 65, 68

McConnell, Malcolm, 78
McDonnell Douglas Corp., 49
McNaugher, Thomas L., 69
McVadon, Eric, 80
Manchu Empire, 28
Manglai, Wang, 61
Mao Tse-tung, 29, 52, 54, 71
Marx, Karl, 36
Memorandum of Understanding (MOU),
    14, 17, 18, 61
military, growth of Chinese, 14-15, 21-
    22, 67-68
    and arms control, 74-77
    and dual-use technology, 16, 21
    and espionage by China, 78-82
    and missile sales by China, 14, 21, 41,
        68, 74
    and technology transfer by China, 14,
        41, 68
    United States should prepare for, 69-77
    see also nuclear arms
Ministry of State Security (China), 78
missile sales, Chinese, 14, 21, 41, 68, 74
Missile Technology Control Regime
    (MTCR), 14, 74-77
Mitchell-Pelosi Act (1993), 58
most-favored-nation (MFN) trade status,
    11
    annual renewal of, 27, 57
    Clinton on, 23-25
    linking (conditional) status
        arguments against, 18-21, 24, 34-37,
        50-51
    based on wrong assumption, 74
    should be maintained for stronger
        China, 26-29
    should be revoked, 52-54
    should not have been renewed, 49-50
MOU (Memorandum of Understanding),
    14, 17, 18, 61
MTCR (Missile Technology Control
    Regime), 14, 74-77
Munro, Ross, 18
Murray, Douglas, 15

National Committee on United States-
    China Relations, 20
National Defense University (Beijing),
    38

NATO (North Atlantic Treaty
  Organization), 71
Newkirk, Douglas, 17
New York Times, 50, 58
Nixon, Richard, 53-54
Non-Proliferation Treaty (NPT), 40,
  74-75
North American Free Trade Agreement
  (NAFTA), 31, 51
North Atlantic Treaty Organization
  (NATO), 71
North Korea
  as nuclear threat, 15, 36, 40, 72
nuclear arms
  China as nuclear threat, 80-81
  China's testing against ban, 53
  North Korea as nuclear threat, 15, 36,
    40, 72
  technology transfer by China, 14, 41,
    68

O'Leary, Hazel, 64
Olympics, China's desire to host, 17
"One China Policy," 17
Outer Mongolia, 71
Outer Space Treaty (1984), 74

Paal, Douglas, 81
Pacific Basin Import-Export Co., 78, 79
Patten, Christopher, 18
Pelosi, Nancy, 80
Peña, Federico, 68
Penny, J.C., 49
Perry, William, 38
piracy. *See* intellectual property rights
political prisoners, 20, 35, 56, 59-61
Pressler, Larry, 80
prison labor, Chinese, 14, 23, 61-62
The Progressive, 49
Puebla Institute, 35, 37

Qian Qiche, 35

Rabin, Yitzhak, 32
Radio Free Asia, 24
Ramos, Fidel V., 72
Reagan, Ronald, 34
Red Cross, 27, 59

sanctions, against China, 58
Sears, 49
security
  Asian, 39-41
  Asia-Pacific, 38-43
Shanghai Automotive Industry
  Corporation, 66
Shattuck, John, 60
Shengjian Motorcycle Factory, 62
Singapore, 13

Smith, Chris, 65
South China Sea, 21, 71-73
South Korea
  and China, 13
  importance to U.S., 40-41
Spratly and Paracel Islands, 15, 71-73
State Council Intellectual Property
  Enforcement Action Plan, 45
"Statement of Cooperation on the
  Implementation of the MOU," 61
sterilizations, forced, 65-66
Sun, Lena, 50
Sun Tzu, 43
Sun Yat-sen, 71
Supreme People's Court (China), 45

Taiwan
  and China, 13-14, 21, 28, 41, 73-74
Taiwan Relations Act, 41, 77
Tariff Act (1930), 14
technology
  China's need for, 16
  dual-use, 16, 21
  U.S.-China cooperation on is
    important, 46-47
Tiananmen Square massacre, 12, 21, 24,
  27, 34, 36, 65, 74
Tian Ye, 60
Tibet
  and China, 10
trade
  helps human rights, 36-37
  managed, 18
Trade Act (1974), 48, 58
Triplett, William, II, 75, 82

United Nations
  China's Security Council membership,
    11
  Development Programme (UNDP), 15
  Human Rights Commission, 20, 65
  Working Group on Arbitrary
    Detentions, 59
United States
  and Asian security, 39-40
  cooperation-with-confrontation policy
    toward China, 10-22
  Strengthens Asia-Pacific Security, 38-
    43
  military ties with China, 38-43
  needs China's cooperation on
    intellectual property rights, 44-48
  offshore production in, 13
  as paper tiger, 52
  seeks from China
    economic agenda, 13-14
    international agenda, 14-15
    political agenda, 11-13
    should crack down on Chinese

espionage, 78-82
should prepare for Chinese military threat, 69-77
should stress human rights in China, 55-63
should stress trade with China, 30-33
tolerates China's wrongdoings, 64-68
United States-China Communiqué on Taiwan, 77
United States-Hong Kong Policy Act (1992), 14
U.S.-China Business Council, 18, 32
U.S. Customs Service, 47, 61
U.S. Department of Justice, 47
U.S. Patent and Trademark Office, 47

Valencia, Mark, 72
Varo, Inc., 79
Voice of America, 18, 24

Wang Juntao, 59
Wannall, Raymond, 79, 81

Washington Post, 50
Washington Times, 68
Wei Jingsheng, 55-56, 59
Wei Jingyi, 60
World Bank, 15
World Trade Organization, 68
Wu, Henry, 65
Wu Bin, 78-79
Wu Yi, 44

Xiao Biguang, 59
Xi Yang, 60
Xu Huizi, 42

Yeltsin, Boris, 37
Yuan Hongbing, 59

Zhang Pinzhe, 78-79
Zhang Yafei, 61
Zheng Yunsu, 62
Zhou Guoqiang, 60
Zweig, David, 10